The Institute of Biology's
Studies in Biology no. 115

Vocal Communication in Birds

Clive K. Catchpole

B.Sc., Ph.D.
Lecturer in Zoology, Bedford College,
University of London

University Park Press

Baltimore

© Clive K. Catchpole, 1979

First published 1979 by Edward Arnold (Publishers) Limited, London
First published in the USA in 1979 by
University Park Press
233 East Redwood Street
Baltimore, Maryland 21202

Library of Congress Cataloging in Publication Data

Catchpole, Clive.
  Vocal communication in birds.

  (Studies in Biology; 115)
  Bibliography: p.
  1. Birds – Behavior.   2.   Animal communication.
I.   Title.   II.   Series: Institute of Biology.   Studies in Biology; 115.
QL698.3.C37   1980   598.2'5'9   79-5158

ISBN 0-8391-0266-6

Printed and bound in Great Britain

General Preface to the Series

Because it is no longer possible for one textbook to cover the whole field of biology while remaining sufficiently up to date, the Institute of Biology has sponsored this series so that teachers and students can learn about significant developments. The enthusiastic acceptance of 'Studies in Biology' shows that the books are providing authoritative views of biological topics.

The features of the series include the attention given to methods, the selected list of books for further reading and, wherever possible, suggestions for practical work.

Readers' comments will be welcomed by the Education Officer of the Institute.

1979   Institute of Biology
                                         41 Queen's Gate
                                         London SW7 5HU

Preface

Man has always been fascinated by the elaborate and often very beautiful vocalizations produced by birds. Writings of the early naturalists, as well as poets and philosophers, concentrated upon the descriptive, aesthetic and musical aspects of songs. During the late 1950s, advancing technology resulted in the development and use of equipment which at last put the subject on to an objective, scientific basis. Since then, interest and research into all aspects of vocal communication in birds has continued to expand, and for this reason I have had to be selective rather than comprehensive in compiling this short introduction to the subject. In doing so, I have favoured studies which are analytical and functional rather than merely descriptive, and in particular I have tried to emphasize the experimental approach both in laboratory and field. The underlying theme of the book is not only to show how birds communicate with their vocalizations, but also to suggest wherever possible why they have been selected for during evolution. In spite of considerable advances in recent years, the central problem of why birds have evolved such complex and varied vocalizations remains one of the most interesting, challenging and elusive questions in the field of animal communication.

London, 1979   C. K. C.

Contents

1 The Communication System

Although most people would probably agree that animals communicate with one another, there is rather less agreement about how and why they do it, and sometimes a tendency to compare the world of animal communication with that of human language. *Communication* is rather a difficult term to define, but in general it is the process whereby the behaviour of one animal alters the probability of some behaviour in another. During communication, information is passed between animals by signalling, but it is not enough to merely detect the signal. For the scientist to establish that communication has really occurred it must also be shown that the signal has in some way altered the behaviour of the recipient. SMITH (1965) has also pointed out that there is a clear distinction between the message contained in the signal and its actual meaning to a recipient. The message may remain constant, but its meaning may vary with context and receiver. For example, many birds sing in territory, but whereas the song means 'keep out' to a rival male it means 'come in' to a female. Most traditional views of animal communication emphasize the sharing of information between individuals to their mutual advantage. A more recent view, put forward by DAWKINS and KREBS (1978), is that during evolution the signaller has been selected to manipulate and exploit the behaviour of other individuals to his own advantage. Any communication system must have a sender, a signal, a medium and a receiver, and the general principles underlying communication apply to all animals. In this book we will be dealing with only one type of communication – acoustic – in one group of animals – birds. Although they use other methods to produce sounds, those produced by their vocal apparatus are some of the most complex known in any animal group, including humans. Whether bird *vocalizations* are in any way analogous to human *language* is extremely doubtful, but they do represent the evolution of an extremely sophisticated communication system which we are only just beginning to understand.

1.1 Sound production

Sound waves are alternating changes in the pressure of the medium, which is normally air. The height, or *amplitude*, of sound waves are measured in microbars, but a more familiar unit which measures sound volume is the *decibel* (dB), a logarithmic scale of pressure ratios. *Wavelength* measures the distance in millimetres of one complete wave alternation or cycle, and the number of cycles per second is known as the *frequency*. Frequency is normally measured in units of thousand cycles or *kiloHertz* (kHz), and gives an indication of how high or low sound is pitched.

Birds produce sounds in many different ways, clapping the wings together, snapping the bill, and of course the well-known drumming of woodpeckers. Interesting as these sounds are, they are still relatively primitive compared to those produced by their vocal apparatus, the *syrinx*. The syrinx contains special membranes which, due to the passage of air forced over them, vibrate and so generate sound waves. Humans and other mammals produce sounds from the larynx situated at the top of the trachea, but in birds the syrinx is much lower at the junction of the two bronchi. There is considerable variation in syrinx structure, but passerine birds, which include the oscines or true song birds, have the most complex of all. The *tympaniform membranes* are situated on the bronchial walls and vibrate as air is forced over them in each bronchial lumen. Several pairs of syringeal muscles act to control membrane tension and thus vary the quality of sounds produced. The most obvious differences between this system and a mammal larynx is that there are two quite separate sound sources, one in each bronchus. That the two sources might produce separate sounds has long been suspected, as two harmonically unrelated sounds which clearly overlap in time have been detected on the sonagram (see § 2.2) traces of several species. NOTTEBOHM (1971) was able to confirm this experimentally on the chaffinch (*Fringilla coelebs*) by severing the right or left hypoglossal motor nerves which supply the right and left sides of the syrinx. Birds which have the right side denervated and are allowed to recover lose only one or two elements from the song, whereas those denervated on the left side lose practically all the elements leaving only one or two (Fig. 1–1). It seems that although each side

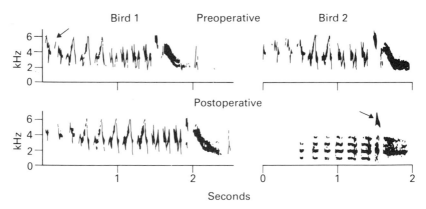

Fig. 1–1   Two male chaffinches shared the same song type, then bird 1 had the right hypoglossus cut and lost one song element (arrowed) while 2 had the left hypoglossus cut and lost all but one element (arrowed). (The unstructured sounds in 2's song are a result of airflow through the denervated bronchus.) (From NOTTEBOHM, 1971.)

normally produces a part of the complete song, the left side predominates and is responsible for most of it. This *lateralization* of control has since been confirmed in other species, but to what extent the intact bird synchronizes or independently controls output from both bronchi during normal singing is unknown. It is now thought that this lateralization may extend to the central nervous system (CNS) where attempts are being made to investigate the central control of vocalizations. If it does, there is an intriguing parallel with the control of human speech where cerebral dominance by one hemisphere also occurs.

1.2   Hearing

The outer ear of birds is not very obvious, due to the absence of an external pinna. This is thought to be for aerodynamic reasons, although bats which also fly usually have a large external pinna. The opening of the *external auditory meatus* is protected by feathers which, although they may hinder hearing, to some extent are essential to reduce wind noise during flight. The meatus conducts sound to the *tympanic membrane* or eardrum which vibrates due to changes in pressure. The middle ear transmits these changes mechanically to the inner ear. In birds this is done by a single bone, the *columella* unlike the three ear ossicles of mammals. The columella is held by ligaments against an oval window to the fluid-filled *cochlea* of the inner ear. It is here that sensory hair cells act as the final transducers of mechanical vibrations into nerve impulses. The cochlea is a tube which has a much folded roof, the *tegmentum vasculosum*, which covers the *basilar membrane*. Pressure changes cause the basilar membrane to vibrate and the sensory hair cells to discharge nerve impulses to the brain. It has long been suspected that different sound frequencies excite different regions of the basilar membrane. In birds, the length of the cochlea and basilar membrane is much shorter than in mammals, which may mean that the CNS plays a more important role in frequency perception. The frequency range to which the ear is sensitive varies from species to species, but the area of maximum sensitivity generally appears to be between 1 and 4 kHz (Fig. 1–2), much the same as in man. Early methods of determining frequency ranges relied solely upon behavioural audibility curves obtained in conditioning experiments. Later techniques used cochlear potentials, and now potentials can be recorded from the *cochlear nuclei*, groups of neurones in the brain itself. KONISHI (1970) has applied this technique to several species, and found that the threshold curves obtained closely match those found by earlier behavioural studies (Fig. 1–2). His neurophysiological studies have also confirmed that birds cannot hear high (*ultrasonic*) frequencies beyond the audible range of humans, above about 20 kHz. Although birds do produce ultrasonic sound (THORPE and GRIFFIN, 1962), it is of low intensity and always associated with audible sounds. MOSS and LOCKIE (1979) have recently shown that capercaillies (*Tetrao urogallus*) produce very low (*infrasonic*) frequencies

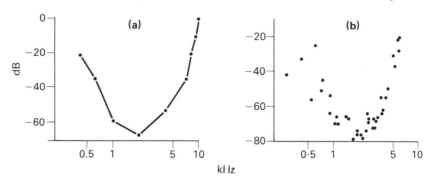

Fig. 1–2   A behavioural audibility curve (a) compared to neural thresholds (b) obtained from the brain of a starling (*Sturnus vulgaris*). (From KONISHI, 1970.)

inaudible to humans, below 40 Hz, but there is as yet no evidence that they can hear it themselves.

It has already been mentioned that the avian cochlea is much shorter than in mammals, but it is also broader and contains more sensory hair cells per unit length of basilar membrane. Another difference is the extensive folding of the tegmentum vasculosum which is thought to have a damping effect bringing the system to rest more quickly. It has often been suggested that such design might well improve the *temporal resolution* of sounds which follow one another quickly. Even cursory examination of sonagrams shows that birds usually produce as many as ten distinct syllables per second, and also extremely rapid frequency modulations. Evidence will be presented in later chapters to show that birds are quite capable of discriminating between such minute variations particularly in the temporal patterning of calls and songs. Neurophysiological evidence of high temporal resolution of sounds has been obtained by KONISHI (1969) from the cochlear nuclei of the brain. Single clicks were resolved with intervals between them of only about 2 ms and sometimes less. Behavioural evidence has now been obtained by WILKINSON and HOWSE (1975) who trained captive birds to discriminate between double and single clicks for a food reward. They could still resolve double clicks as two separate sounds when the click interval was as small as 2 milliseconds. Such powers of resolution are way beyond those of most mammals including man, and it does seem that birds are capable of communicating with sounds on a much faster time scale than humans.

2 Methods and Techniques

There are many different levels at which the investigation of vocalizations can proceed. The first step is to find a singing bird and be able to hear it clearly. By listening carefully and taking detailed notes, the early naturalists were able to describe many important features and characteristics of the different species' vocalizations. However, subjective descriptions based upon memory and recorded in verbal shorthand are of little use to the modern scientist, who needs to make an accurate record of the vocalizations. Tape recordings can be repeatedly analysed by modern electronic equipment to reveal the precise details of vocalization structure for comparison and further study. It may also give clues as to function, a hypothesis can be set up, and a series of experiments planned to test it. These may involve captive birds in the laboratory or playback experiments on natural populations in the wild.

2.1 Sound recording

The recording equipment must satisfy the following criteria. It should be of high quality for later laboratory analysis of recordings, and yet be light, portable and robust for work in the field. With the advent of solid-state physics and miniaturization, there is now a reasonable choice of such equipment, some of it specially designed with the above requirements in mind. A battery-operated tape recorder with an adequate *frequency response* and high tape speed is essential to capture the rapid frequency modulations mentioned earlier.

Selection of the correct type of microphone is extremely important, and for most work a *dynamic microphone* is best. Several are now designed specifically for outside work and so are suitably robust as well as being sensitive and responsive to the frequency ranges described earlier. Since they mostly have low impedance, long cables can be used if necessary to connect with the tape recorder input. There are only two ways of getting close enough to obtain a good quality recording: positioning the microphone near the singing bird at the end of a long cable, or using a parabolic reflector and microphone some distance away.

The *parabolic reflector* has undoubtedly made the collection of good quality recordings much easier, and is indispensable to the modern recordist. It consists of a shallow dish, which when pointed at a distant sound source reflects the sound waves and concentrates them to a focal point. The microphone is positioned facing into the dish at the focal point (Fig. 2–1) and so receives the greatly amplified sound. The reflector also makes the system more directional and selective by cutting down on

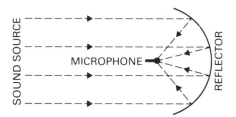

Fig. 2-1 Diagrammatic representation of a parabolic reflector to show the positioning of a microphone at the focal point of sound-wave reflection.

unwanted side noise so improving the signal-to-noise ratio of the whole system. The dish can be accurately directed on to the sound source either by sight, or by wearing headphones and acoustically monitoring the sound input. Dishes come in a variety of sizes, the larger the more powerful, and are made of either aluminium or fibre glass for lightness. They have some disadvantages in wind, and overall frequency response is far from uniform, but generally the advantages more than compensate. An excellent review of different recording techniques and equipment has been published by GULLEDGE(1977).

2.2 Sound analysis and sonagrams

The cathode-ray *oscilloscope* can be used to display recorded sound as a series of waves on the screen. These can be photographed at intervals and then measured to determine frequency and amplitude. There are, however, a number of disadvantages in analysis by oscilloscope, mainly due to the rapid rate of frequency and amplitude modulation in bird vocalizations. To be sure that all the changes are detected, minute sections, measured in fractions of a second, must be displayed and photographed one after the other, before a composite song can be constructed and studied. Oscillographic methods are better suited to the study of sounds which remain fairly constant and for this reason are most often used in the study of insect sound communication.

The development of a special *frequency spectrum analyser*, called a *sonagraph*, revolutionized the study of bird vocalizations. Its potential was soon realized by Thorpe, who was the first to use it extensively on passerine songs. Now available in a variety of forms and with various accessories, its basic principles remain the same. The sonagraph re-records on a magnetic drum a short sample of about 2.5 seconds of the sound to be analysed. It is then rapidly scanned by being revolved and replayed over 500 times through a filter which is gradually tuned to higher frequencies. As this is done, a dark trace is produced on sensitive white paper which is also revolved on a cylinder connected to the drum. The main result of this is to produce a graph of frequency against time, but amplitude is also represented as the darker the shading the greater the amplitude. The trace is called a *sonagram* and may be stored as it is, traced, photocopied or photographed and a great deal of information obtained later by measurement. The main criticism levelled at the sonagraph is that if incorrectly calibrated, used or interpreted, it can give misleading information, but this surely applies to any scientific instrument. Another criticism is that by displaying in detail the extensive minutiae of frequency variations, it actually confuses by giving too much information. This rather curious criticism can be remedied by simplifying the final trace, and obscuring the finer details of harmonic structure and amplitude variations by Indian ink. Many feel that such a simplified trace, which merely shows frequency range and modulations in uniform black, gives sufficient information, particularly for illustrations in books. The main advantage of sonagrams is that they really do give the reader a picture of what sounds are like, and after a little practice even a novice is able to read them with far greater ease than learning musical notation. By actually presenting an objective representation of the recorded sound itself, the sonagram also renders obsolete the necessity to resort to inadequate phonetic descriptions. Although sometimes useful for field ornithologists there are very real dangers of placing any reliance upon these for serious scientific research. In her book, JELLIS (1977) points out how field guides in different countries give remarkably different phonetic descriptions for the same species. The call of the golden oriole (*Oriolus oriolus*) is given as 'weela-weeo' in England, 'tuolio' in France and 'dudelio' in Germany. Upon actually hearing the call from a wild golden oriole for the first time she felt that none of them had given her much help in identifying it. In looking at a sonagram for the first time the reader may experience a similar feeling, and so at this stage here are a few useful hints as to the interpretation of some common vocalizations shown in Fig. 2–2. All these sounds are found in the songs of one single male sedge warbler (*Acrocephalus schoenobaenus*), and are the units, or building blocks, from which songs are constructed. There is considerable variation and disagreement among scientists as to the correct terminology to use, and they are often referred to as notes or syllables. For the sake of convenience and consistency in this book all sub-units within songs will be called *elements*.

In sonagrams, the axis is frequency, measured in kiloHertz (kHz). As frequency approximates to pitch, the higher the noise is, the higher it appears on the trace. The time scale along the abscissa is usually in seconds. Perhaps the most common sound people associate with birds is a whistle. If you make a short whistle of constant pitch, it will appear as a pure, *unmodulated frequency* on the sonagram, a fairly straight horizontal band (**a**). A whistle which starts at a higher frequency and drops to a lower one is said to be *frequency modulated* and appears as a slope (**b**). If more rapid modulations are introduced as in a slow (**c**) or fast (**d**) vibrato, they will be shown on the sonagram. A completely different sound is the harsh

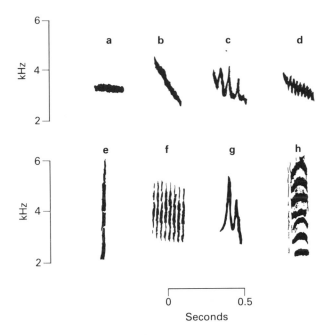

Fig. 2–2   Sonagrams of some different sounds (elements) produced by a male
sedge warbler and described in the text.

noise produced when a wide frequency spectrum is used. A short burst of
wide frequency noise results in a single click (**e**) and if several occur close
together a harsh buzzing or rattling is produced (**f**). Frequency
modulations can occur in a wide variety of complex forms and many will
be encountered later, but (**g**) for example sounds rather like a chirp.
Another complication is when a sound which has a low *fundamental
frequency* also has higher frequencies which occur as multiples of the
fundamental. These are called *harmonics* and in the example here (**h**) result
in a rather gruff barking noise.

There are a number of new instruments which have appeared since the
sonagraph. The *melograph* plots only the main or fundamental frequency
as a single line, but also plots amplitude beneath. A *continuous frequency
spectrum analyser* can now quickly produce sonagram-like traces on an
oscilloscope screen. These can be photographed every few seconds to
greatly speed up what has been a much slower process on the orthodox
sonagraph.

2.3   Experiments

Many laboratory experiments are concerned with the role of *auditory
feedback* in the development of song. Young birds are often taken from the

nest and then raised by hand in aviaries away from other birds. A better, but more difficult form of acoustic isolation, is to hatch and raise the young in special sound-proof chambers. These ensure more complete control of the acoustic environment, and often have built-in microphones and speakers for various experiments. Drastic experiments to remove auditory feedback altogether, involve deafening young birds after hatching by cochlea removal. The results of these methods will be discussed in Chapter 5, but important as laboratory experiments are for song development, they tell us little about the functions of song in the wild.

The most common type of field experiment now performed is the *playback experiment* where an extension speaker is placed in or near territory. It relies upon the well-known tendency of a bird in territory to defend it by showing aggressive behaviour towards the sight or sound of a rival male. Although models and preserved birds can also be used, the use of a recorded acoustic stimulus by itself has the advantage of removing other variables from the experimental design. If a strong *baseline response* to normal recorded song is elicited, then presumably the bird is recognizing and responding to specific features contained in it. Experiments can then proceed to investigate these by varying those features in a variety of ways. A series of pilot experiments will show how a particular species responds to playback and the most appropriate criteria can then be selected. For example, a typical response of a very reactive bird might involve immediately stopping any other behaviour, orientating towards the speaker, approaching it and finally even contacting it. It may also produce vocalizations and visual threat displays. At the simplest level, the response could be scored on an 'all or nothing' basis, but usually each of the different categories are scored separately. They can also be ranked, so that a bird which approaches the speaker scores more than one which merely orientates towards it, and so on. Useful as scoring methods are, they do involve subjective factors, and if possible the best method is to *quantify* responses by *objective measurements*. Ideally several different categories of behaviour should be measured, and this has been done in the example shown in Fig. 2–3.

Five categories were selected to measure the responses of ten male sedge warblers to 4 min of playback of their species song both before and after pairing (CATCHPOLE, 1977). *Latency of response* (**a**) was the reaction time measured from the start of the experimental song to the first movement of the whole bird towards the speaker. As can be seen, this increased significantly after pairing. *Time spent searching* within a 1 m radius of the speaker (**b**) was totalled and this showed a significant decrease after pairing. *Time spent singing* during the 4 min (**c**) showed the most dramatic change, as no males sang after pairing. The *nearest distance* each bird eventually approached to the speaker (**d**) was measured to within 1 m, and this also showed an increase. However, the *number of calls* given (**e**) showed a significant increase after pairing. We will not attempt to draw any conclusions from the experiment at this stage, but it does illustrate how

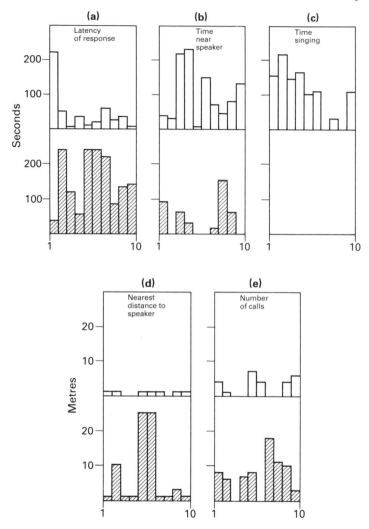

Fig. 2–3 Results obtained by using five different categories of response in the same playback experiment on ten male sedge warblers (1 to 10) before (unshaded) and after (shaded) pairing (From CATCHPOLE, 1977.)

different criteria and methods of measurement give different results. More sophisticated methods and measurements may involve several observers, the use of additional tape recorders and film cameras. Experimental design, categories of response, methods of measurement and appropriate statistical tests, should all be planned together to achieve meaningful results.

3 Calls and Communication

Bird vocalizations are traditionally divided into calls and songs, and although there are considerable difficulties in exactly defining the two terms, the distinction still remains a useful one. As a general rule, *songs* are long, more complex in structure and produced by males in the breeding season, whereas *calls* are short, simple and produced by both sexes throughout the year. As we will see later, there is still considerable debate as to the possible functions of songs, but for several reasons the functional interpretation of calls is less difficult and so provides a useful starting point.

3.1 The functions of calls

One reason why the functions of calls are better understood, is that they are given in quite specific *contexts* or during certain behaviour patterns. Any variation in calling rate, intensity, or sometimes the occurrence of an intermediate form, probably reflect underlying changes in motivation which may also be transmitted to other individuals. If a particular call is only given during territorial displays and fighting, it seems reasonable to assume it is an aggressively motivated threat call. Furthermore, if the call itself is seen to effect the behaviour of other members of the species, then it fulfils our criteria of communication, as well as providing additional clues as to function. Indeed, one characteristic of calls is that in many cases they do have an immediate effect upon the behaviour of other individuals. Calls can be thought of as expressing a tendency to behave in a certain way, and also transmitting that information to other individuals who upon receiving it may modify their behaviour accordingly.

By studying different calls in relation to behaviour, it has been possible to build up the total *vocabulary* of calls for many species. THORPE (1961) has tabulated data from several species and it can be seen (Table 1) that the size of call vocabulary varies considerably from species to species. Passerines, on average, have a rather larger vocabulary than other groups, but overall there seems to be an upper limit of about 15 different calls in any one vocabulary. In most cases there is room for at least one call for flight or aggression, but as many as three calls for different alarm and courtship situations. The young too have their own special calls, such as when begging food from their parents. The various categories presented by Thorpe in his summary give a good idea of the overall range and type of calls to be found in most bird vocabularies.

However, these categories are not comprehensive, and there are also

Table 1   The call vocabularies of various species. (From THORPE, 1961.)

Circumstances in which uttered	Herring gull	Fowl	Dove	Great tit	Chaffinch	Buntings	Blackbird	Whitethroat	Pied flycatcher	Wren	Song sparrow
Calls of adults											
Flight	.	.	.	+	+	+	+	+	.	.	+
Settling	.	.	+	+	.	.	.	+	.	.	.
Social (flock)	+(2)	.	+	+	+	|	|	+	+	+	+
Alarm 1	+	+	+	+	+	+	+	+	+	+	+
Alarm 2	.	.	.	.	+	+	+	+	+	+	+
Alarm 3	.	.	.	.	+	+	+	+	+	+	+
Flying predator	.	.	.	+	+	.	+	.	+	+	.
Ground predator	.	+	.	+	+	.	+	?	.	+	+
Distress scream	.	+	+	.	+	.	+	.	+	+	+(2)
Aggressive	+	+	+	.	+	+	.	+	+	+	+
Territorial	.	+	.	.	.	.	+	+	+	.	+
Courtship 1	.	.	+	+	+	+	+	+	.	+	+
Courtship 2	.	.	.	.	+	.	.	+	.	+	+
Courtship 3	.	.	.	.	+	.	.	+	.	.	.
Copulation	+	.	+	+	+	+	.	+	.	+	+
Nest-site	.	.	+	.	.	+	.	.	+	.	+
Mate feeding	+	.	.	+	.	+	.	?	.	.	.
Food	+	+	.	.	.	.	.	.	.	.	.
Roosting	.	.	.	.	.	.	+	?	.	+	.
Total	7	6	8	9	13	10	11	12 (or 15)	9	12	14
Calls of young											
Pleasure	.	+	.	.	.	.	.	.	.	.	.
Distress	.	+	.	.	.	.	+	+	.	.	+
Distant begging	.	.	.	.	+	+	+	+	+	.	+
Close begging	.	.	.	.	+	+	+	+	+	+	+
	.	2	.	.	2	2	3	3	2	1	3
Total	7	8	8	9	15	12	14	15 (or 18)	11	13	17

calls which have more unusual and highly specialized functions. These may involve communicating with other species, *interspecific communication*, or using calls as a form of sonar, *autocommunication*. One particularly interesting example is shown by African honeyguides, such as the aptly named *Indicator indicator*, whose special calls and behaviour guide men and other mammals to the nests of wild honeybees. The nests, which would otherwise be inaccessible to the birds, are broken into by the larger animal, and the honeyguides can then feed on broken pieces of the comb. This symbiotic relationship appears to have developed originally between the birds and honey-eating badgers called ratels. Later, African tribesmen also searching for honey learned to follow and take advantage of the persistent calling birds. Although the behaviour of calling and leading may be largely innate, the honeyguide must presumably learn how to find bees' nests, and also which animals to approach and guide. Similarly, the predator must learn to associate following the calling bird with eventually finding prey if the communication system is to work effectively. There is some evidence that as the more sophisticated Africans lose interest in searching for wild honey, the honeyguides in some areas no longer react to humans and guide them as they did before.

Another unusual example is the use of special calls by various cave-dwelling birds, such as the oil bird (*Steatornis caripensis*) from South America, and cave swiftlets of the genus *Collocalia* from South East Asia. These birds produce a series of clicks when flying in darkness, and appear to have an echo-locating *sonar* system similar to that possessed by bats. Unlike bats, the calls are not ultrasonic, but produced at normal frequencies and so can be clearly heard by humans. In the oil bird, the clicks are produced in darkness, and in short bursts with intervals of a few milliseconds between them. When landing on a dark cave ledge the click rate increases, but if a torch is switched on, it decreases or stops altogether. Oil birds fly safely in darkened experimental rooms, but if the ears are plugged they crash into the walls. Cave swiftlets increase their rate of click production as they penetrate deeper into their dark caves. GRIFFIN and SUTHERS (1970) found that in a darkened experimental room *Collocalia vanikorensis* produces clicks between 4.5 and 7.5 kHz (Fig. 3–1) and can

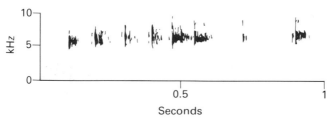

Fig. 3–1   Echo-locating clicks produced by the cave swiftlet (*Collocalia vanikorensis*). (From GRIFFIN and SUTHERS, 1970.)

avoid wires as small as 6 mm in diameter. The special sonar system is obviously an adaptation which allows these species to colonize and breed successfully in the shelter of dark caves. It also suggests that the birds are capable of resolving echoes a few milliseconds apart, a feat which does not seem unlikely considering the evidence presented earlier on auditory time resolution in birds (see § 1.2). Whether the clicks which have a relatively wide frequency range are used in intraspecific communication as well as navigation is not known, but the relationship between this design of call and directional information will be considered in the following section.

3.2   Alarm calls

Many calls appear to be associated with fear and danger. These vary from general distress calls, to special *alarm calls* which only occur in response to a particular type of predator. *Distress calls* are high-intensity calls given when birds are held during trapping, attacked by a predator or injured. Because they are very loud it is possible that they might startle or confuse a predator and enable the captured bird to escape. Playback experiments with distress calls have obtained varying results. In some cases they result in other individuals dispersing, and for this reason have been used against gulls and crows at airports where they constitute a bird-strike hazard.

Similarities among the alarm calls of different passerine species have been emphasized by MARLER (1957) who provided an elegant explanation relating their basic design to the omission of certain types of information. In the case of a flying hawk predator, although it is advantageous for small birds to warn their mate, offspring or kin, it is obviously disadvantageous to give their own position away by calling. There is a conflict between being conspicuous to other individuals and yet remaining inconspicuous to a predator. The conflict has been resolved by the evolution of special *flying predator calls* which can be clearly heard, but which transmit a *minimum of directional information* and are difficult to locate. Birds and humans are thought to locate sounds by binaural comparisons of *phase*, intensity and time differences. Phase differences are more effective at low frequencies, as the information becomes ambiguous when wavelength is less than twice the distance between the two receiving ears. Conversely, *intensity* differences are more effective at high frequencies, because the sound shadow formed by the head of the listening bird only operates when the head dimension exceeds sound wavelength. *Time* differences are effective throughout the frequency range, but are enhanced by interruption, repetition and modulation. The further apart the ears of the listening bird, the more obvious time differences will become. Rough calculations suggest that for a medium-sized bird of prey, a call pitched at about 7 kHz would be too high for detectable phase differences, and too low for an appreciable sound shadow intensity effect. As Fig. 3–2 shows, this is just the frequency range of the special alarm calls many passerines produce when a real or experimental hawk flies over. Any possibility of binaural time differences are minimized by the almost imperceptible gradual start and finish. Modulations are minimal, there are generally no interruptions and the calls are not repeated close together. They appear to be a classic example of *convergent evolution* in an acoustic signal which has become finely tuned within these narrow constraints to achieve the same objective in different families of passerine birds. To human listeners the calls sound much the same – a high, thin whistle which is easy to hear but extremely difficult to

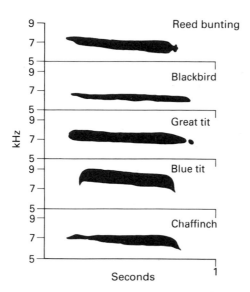

Fig. 3–2   The calls given by five different species when a hawk flies overhead. (From MARLER, 1957.)

locate. It has always been assumed that birds of prey would have similar difficulty, but SHALTER (1978) has now shown that under experimental conditions several species appear to be able to orientate towards the source of this type of call. What possible advantage an individual obtains by giving such a call and possibly decreasing his own chances of survival has always been the subject of intense debate. Whether the behaviour really is an example of altruistic behaviour, whether kin selection is involved, or whether the signaller really deceives the hawk or even other individuals in the flock, have all been suggested. Shalter's recent findings will certainly pose problems for those who have always assumed that the calls cannot be located or only with great difficulty by birds of prey. But it should also be borne in mind that just because some species of hawk *now* have the ability to locate the calls, this may not always have been the case when they were first shaped by natural selection. Furthermore, their design may still make the task of location more difficult or time-consuming in at least some cases in the wild.

With a stationary predator, such as an owl discovered perching in the daytime, there is less immediate danger and so directional information can be given. In these circumstances another special alarm call is given by each species, but one which has quite a different structure (Fig. 3–3). The calls share another common design, which this time is almost the converse of the earlier one as it carries *directional information*. To facilitate this the calls are short, start and finish abruptly, cover a wide frequency range, may be modulated, and are often repeated. The wide frequency ranges

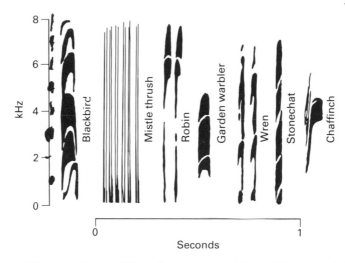

Fig. 3-3   The calls of seven different species given while mobbing an owl. (From
MARLER, 1957.)

provide ample clues for phase and intensity differences, whereas sudden
starts, stops and repetition provide clues for time differences. The sounds
are loud, harsh, often repeated clicks, which are easy to locate compared
with the high, thin whistle of the flying predator calls. Upon hearing
them, other individuals and species use the directional information and
are often attracted. They then form into large mobbing parties which
harass and confuse the unfortunate owl.

Alarm calls which share these basic designs appear to be beautifully
adapted to fulfil a particular function. The calls also maintain a certain
degree of *specific distinctiveness*, each species giving its own particular
version of a basic call. It may be that there is a balance between
conforming to the basic design which also permits interspecific
communication, yet still maintaining some degree of specific
distinctiveness for intraspecific communication. In the flying predator
call, specific distinctiveness has been almost abandoned, and the calls of
quite unrelated species transmit a general alarm with minimal additional
information. The owl-mobbing calls, with their greater frequency range,
modulations and repetitions give additional information concerning
location, and possibly species too.

3.3   Calls and individual recognition

It is now clear that any one call may transmit several quite different
types of information at the same time. As we have seen, some alarm calls
may indicate not only the presence of a particular type of predator in the
area, but also the species of the caller, and where he is calling from. There

is now evidence from a number of species, that a call may also contain enough information to transmit the identity of a particular individual too. Furthermore, it can also be shown that others in the population react to such calls in a manner which suggests that they are quite capable of *individual recognition* by sound alone. Many observers have noted the apparent ease with which parents returning with food locate their young in the vast, densely-packed colonies of breeding seabirds. The very fact that parents feed and maintain their young in family groups, and not on a communal basis, suggests that individual recognition must occur. Although visual information may play some part in this, most parents give special calls well before landing and the young react before the parent actually appears.

TSCHANZ (1968), working on the guillemot (*Uria aalge*), was the first to demonstrate individual recognition by sound in a colonial seabird. To obtain positive proof of recognition, two things must be demonstrated. First, the calls must be *individually distinct* to form a physical basis, and secondly, the mate or young must *react significantly more* to the particular call of their mate or parent than to the calls of other individuals. Tschanz was able to demonstrate both in the guillemot, and used two types of playback experiment to confirm recognition. In one, presentation of the parental call alternated with a control call, and in the other a choice was given by presenting the call simultaneously with the control call using two speakers. In both cases the results were quite clear, the young birds responded only to the calls of their parents. Measures of response included orientation to the speaker, approach, contact, pecking at it as though begging for food, and giving calls. Control calls from other adults or chicks usually resulted in staying or going into hiding and actually avoiding the speaker.

Tschanz also attempted to study the possible development of parent–young recognition by playing back adult calls to eggs in incubators during the last few days prior to hatching. After hatching they were given a choice test, and in most cases approached only the speaker transmitting the calls to which they had been exposed in the egg. Control chicks from an incubator with no playback approached both speakers alternately. It does seem that early exposure whilst still in the egg enhances the *early learning* of parental calls which may also continue to develop in the first few days after hatching. Acoustic stimuli clearly have an advantage over visual stimuli, as discrimination learning can start with the embryo prior to hatching. Acoustic communication between eggs and parents no longer seems unlikely since the work of VINCE (1969) on *embryonic communication* between the developing eggs of certain quail species. The developing eggs within a clutch are in constant acoustic communication by the production of special clicks, and these play an important role in the synchronization of hatching. It used to be thought the clicks were produced by tapping against the shell, but it now seems that they are special calls produced during respiratory movements.

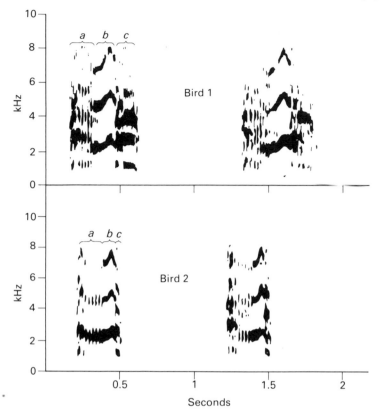

Fig. 3-4 Individual distinctiveness in successive calls from two sandwich terns (From HUTCHINSON *et al.*, 1968.)

Having established the physical basis for recognition and confirmed its presence by playback experiments, it still remained to investigate what particular sound characteristics within the calls are actually used by the birds during recognition. HUTCHINSON, STEVENSON and THORPE (1968) soon demonstrated that the calls of sandwich terns (*Sterna sandvicensis*) have remarkably consistent differences between individuals (Fig. 3-4). The calls can be divided into three distinct segments (a, b and c on figure) which vary in *frequency* and *duration* between different individuals to give each bird its own distinctive call pattern. In the landing calls of gannets (*Sula bassana*), no such clear differences are apparent from sonagrams, and yet there is good evidence for individual recognition. WHITE and WHITE (1970) used film cameras linked to playback experiments and confirmed that sitting birds in the colony only reacted to the landing calls of their respective mates. Following amplitude analysis it emerged that each bird had its own quite distinct pattern or *amplitude profile* (Fig. 3-5).

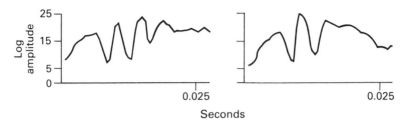

Seconds

Fig. 3–5 Individual distinctiveness in the average amplitude profiles of the calls of two male gannets. (From WHITE and WHITE, 1970.)

Furthermore, it appears that the individual distinctiveness resides in the very first few peaks and troughs. For each individual an average amplitude profile was constructed which clearly reveals the extent of the variations between them. The calls are so consistent in any one individual that only about the first tenth of a second is needed in theory for recognition to occur.

Individual recognition by calls is obviously important in colonial seabirds but by no means restricted to them. The development of complex songs in passerine birds affords ample scope for acoustic recognition as we will see later, but it would be surprising if their extensive call vocabularies were not also involved. MUNDINGER (1970) has now discovered that in the American goldfinch (*Carduelis tristis*) an extremely subtle form of individual recognition has developed. Each mated pair shares its own distinct version of the species flight call which is used particularly during the breeding cycle (Fig. 3–6). Playback experiments confirm that recognition occurs, and also that during

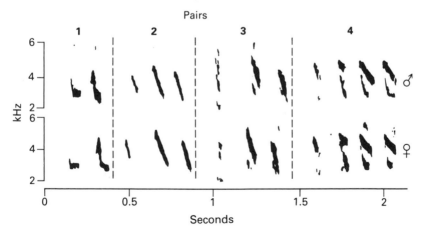

Fig. 3–6 Individually distinct calls shared within four pairs of American goldfinches. (From MUNDINGER, 1970.)

pairing the special call is *learned* by one of the pair *imitating* a call already in the vocabulary of the other. Calls, unlike songs are generally regarded as inherited, but clearly some species possess the ability to modify and extend their vocabulary by later learning, in this case to facilitate individual recognition within the mated pair.

4 Song and Communication

As shown in the previous chapter, it seems that even quite simple calls are capable of carrying several different types of information. The more familiar songs of passerine birds have a longer and more complicated structure, and so in theory at least have the *potential* to carry even more information. Songs are often so complex and variable that modern researchers are only just beginning to analyse their detailed structures, set up hypotheses about their possible functions and test them out by playback experiments in the field. Quite a few species have been investigated in this way, but so far the findings have given no clear, simple answers or general rules as in a code or language. Indeed, it now seems highly unlikely that bird songs are in any way analogous to human language, and we should be wary of making even simple assumptions, such as that longer or more complex songs are necessarily correlated with more complicated types of information or functions. We have seen in Chapter 1 that the information transfer may be taking place on a very fast time scale. We will now see that birds may be responding to quite different *parameters* of the sound signal from those that the human listener uses when he attempts to recognize the species of the singing bird. These important points have emerged from several experimental studies into how the listening bird recognizes a complicated sound signal as the song of its own species.

4.1 Song and species recognition

One of the first, and certainly most thorough, experimental investigations into species recognition was carried out by BREMOND (1968) on the European robin (*Erithacus rubecula*). The songs of robins are extremely complex consisting of combinations of several different phrases (Fig. 4–1). Each phrase is quite a complicated structure and although only about four appear in a song, each robin has a repertoire of several hundred so the possible permutations become quite astronomical. Straight away it can be seen that there is really no such thing as '*the* song of the robin' – a set pattern of phrases always repeated in the same order. Instead, variability is the keynote and yet Bremond discovered a simple set of rules which appear to underlie their overall song organization. The first rule is that *all the phrases* within a song are different, the second is that in a run of consecutive songs *all the songs* are different, and the third is that *successive phrases* alternate in pitch between high and low frequencies. Just how important this third rule is for species recognition was demonstrated by Bremond in a series of playback

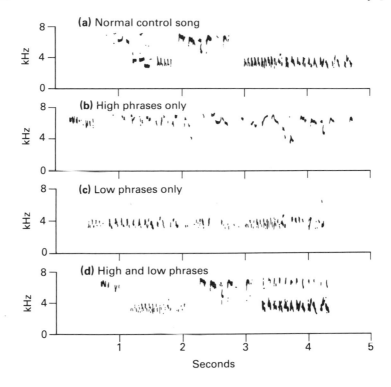

Fig. 4–1 Normal and artificial robin songs used in playback experiments by J. Bremond. (From JELLIS, 1977.)

experiments using *artificially constructed songs*. The artificial songs were of two main types, those made by splicing together real robin phrases in various combinations, and those constructed quite artificially from an electronic sound generator. Bremond scored his responses using a fairly simple method. If the robin showed a strong or moderate response by being attracted close to the speaker it counted as a positive result, and the final number responding was simply expressed as a percentage of the total number used in any one experiment. Bremond was careful to use controls and to calibrate his experimental set-up from the start by studying the reaction to playback of normal robin song. He found that 88% of robins responded and so this is the baseline response against which all other experiments must be compared. By then varying only one parameter at a time and holding all others constant it was possible to gradually reveal which are the most important parameters for species recognition in the robin.

The first experiments used an artificial song made up by repeating just one robin phrase, but no birds responded to this whether it was a high or low frequency phrase. Another experiment used different phrases, but they were all of high frequency (Fig. 4–1b) and the response was 56%. A similar experiment with all different low frequency phrases (Fig. 4–1c) obtained a similar response of 52%. Clearly, the rule that all phrases should be different is quite important for species recognition. However, when normal song was simulated by joining together all different phrases of alternating high and low frequency (Fig. 4–1d) the response of 90% was almost the same as for normal control song (Fig. 4–1a). The alternation rule then, is also extremely important for species recognition in the robin. Perhaps the most interesting conclusion from Bremond's study is that it is not the fine structure of the individual elements within the song that is important, but the overall pattern of its general structure, what he has called *syntax*. Knowing these *syntactical rules* of variation and alternation it should be possible to perform a final test by constructing a totally artificial song from an electronic sound generator and Bremond has also done this.

He started with a continuous sine wave within the normal frequency range, and modulated it to mimic the regular alternation of high and low phrases. This obtained no response at all, perhaps because there are other small syntax rules which apply to the individual phrases which in real robins usually contain repetitions of small, separate elements. When the signal was fragmented to mimic this more accurately (Fig. 4–2a) a response of 31% was then obtained. Getting closer still by introducing more natural variety within phrases (Fig. 4–2b) surprisingly had no additional effect as a response of only 25% was obtained. It was only when many of these synthetic phrases were strung together to mimic the full syntax rules that the response of 70% approached that of control normal song. That an artificial song constructed of purely synthetic elements obtains such a good response is additional evidence that syntax features are more important than the fine structure of individual elements within the robins' song.

Further evidence comes from an experiment in which Bremond

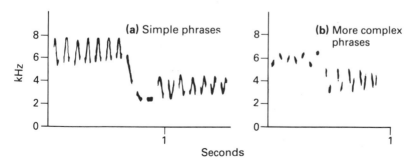

Fig. 4–2   Synthetic robin songs produced by an electronic sound generator. (From BREMOND, 1968.)

inverted the frequency modulation of individual elements, thus completely changing their normal structure, and still obtained a response of 82%.

The somewhat surprising conclusion that syntax features are particularly important in the robin does not necessarily apply to other species. Indeed, as more species are investigated it is becoming clear that different species may respond to quite different parameters, and BREMOND (1976) has recently shown that Bonelli's warbler (*Phylloscopus bonelli*) is a species which contrasts with the robin in many ways. The song is extremely simple and merely consists of the repetition of one element to form a trill of about ten (Fig. 4–3a). The experimental methods were

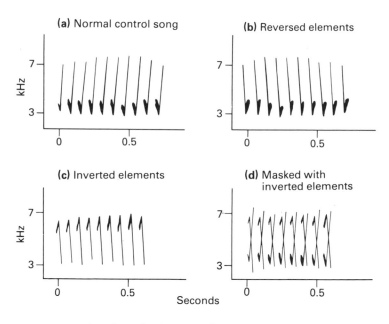

Fig. 4–3   Normal and artificial songs of Bonelli's warbler. (From BREMOND, 1976.)

much the same as for the robin, but here the baseline response to control playback of normal song was 100%. Altering the *element structure* in any way, but particularly its *frequency modulation*, resulted in a greatly reduced response. For example, reversing the elements (Fig. 4–3b) gave a 36% response, and inverting them (Fig. 4–3c) the response dropped to 12% compared to 82% in the similar robin experiment. Even leaving the normal song structure in, but masking it with the inverted frequency modulation, resulted in a drop to 23% (Fig. 4–3d). Clearly in this species the actual structure of the *elements themselves* are of prime importance for species recognition. These experiments only involved quite subtle changes in frequency modulation of the real song elements, but even these resulted in significant changes in response by the listening bird. Bremond also slightly altered the frequency range by transforming the natural song up or down by 1 kHz. Transforming it down had no appreciable effect as the response was 88%, but transforming it up the same amount resulted in a significant drop to 32%. This rather curious difference only makes sense when we consider the ecology of the species and in particular the fact that it is often *sympatric* with the wood warbler (*Phylloscopus sibilatrix*). This species has a similar song which is normally about 1 kHz higher and so to avoid expenditure of unnecessary energy in territorial battles or wasteful hybridization with the wrong species, each has evolved a slightly different sound signal and mechanism for recognition. Bremond calls these rather subtle differences, such as we find here in the small frequency shift, *rejection markers*. The listening Bonelli's warbler immediately rejects the higher frequency song, as shown by the low response, but when the same song was played to wood warblers 50% responded. Recognition of the same species but also efficient rejection of similar and closely related species are some of the important functions of song revealed by these experiments.

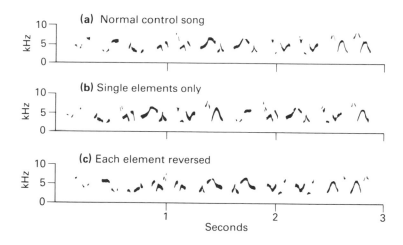

Fig. 4-4   Normal and artificial songs of the indigo bunting. (From EMLEN, 1972.)

Another species which has received considerable attention from American workers in recent years is the indigo bunting (*Passerina cyanea*). EMLEN (1972) and SHIOVITZ (1975) constructed differently ranked scoring systems for their playback experiments and so it is difficult to compare their results directly with those of Bremond. The structure of normal indigo bunting song (Fig. 4-4a) has a very obvious syntax rule in that elements are usually repeated and occur in pairs. Emlen constructed and tested an artificial song (Fig. 4–4b) in which the same elements only appeared singly. The response was almost identical to that obtained from the normal control song, suggesting that syntax is unimportant for recognition in this species. To investigate the importance of element structure he changed it by completely reversing each element within the song without changing their order (Fig. 4–4c). Again he found this made no significant difference. It seems that element structure is also unimportant, but Shiovitz later went on to demonstrate that a lower response is obtained when more subtle structural alterations *within each element* are carried out. The elements contain many up and down frequency modulations and where the change in direction occurs is called the *inflection point*. Shiovitz was able to cut the tape at these inflection points and exchange the segments on either side, thus reversing their order within each element. This time the response was significantly less compared to the control song, suggesting that fine structure is important to some extent. However, the main reason for including the indigo bunting as yet another example is that, unlike the other two species, the rhythm or *temporal patterning* within the song appears to be an important factor in species recognition. This was demonstrated by Emlen who prepared a variety of artificial songs which contained the same elements in the same order, but with different time intervals between them (Fig. 4–5). In this example, the intervals were half and twice as much as the control normal song. In both cases the response obtained was significantly weaker and so demonstrates the importance of temporal patterning for species recognition in the indigo bunting. Bremond performed a similar series of experiments with the robin, but found almost no difference at all. This particular experiment, though relatively simple compared to some, is an excellent example of the technique of varying one parameter whilst holding all others constant.

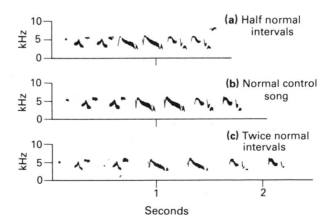

Fig. 4–5   Normal and artificial songs of the indigo bunting. (From EMLEN, 1972.)

In summary, in each species *several parameters* appear to be involved in species recognition, and these differ from species to species in their relative importance. Whatever the features are, if the communication system is to function efficiently then they should be relatively constant within a population, and so far with the species studied this appears to be the case. For example, the time intervals between elements in the indigo bunting population measured by Emlen are remarkably constant and show extremely low coefficients of variation. In the search for parameters important in species recognition, *minimal variation* within a population may be the first and most important clue for the investigator to follow up by later experimental work.

4.2   Song and individual recognition

Although the features of song important in species recognition must remain fairly constant, within this general framework there is still considerable scope for *individual variation*. In many studies it has been shown that each bird within a population may have its own peculiar version of the species song which is quite characteristic. One example is the yellow bunting, usually called the yellowhammer (*Emberiza citrinella*), where each male in a group of adjacent territories has at least one distinctive song of his own (Fig. 4–6). When repeated, the characteristic song structure remains remarkably constant and usually stays so throughout the season and even from year to year. Repetition of a constant signal gives every opportunity for other individuals to learn it and so possibly come to recognize a male as a particular individual within the community.

In Chapter 3, calls and individual recognition were dealt with separately, and concerned recognition between parent and young. The very fact that all information is contained within one call makes the task of identifying the parameters carrying individual information that much

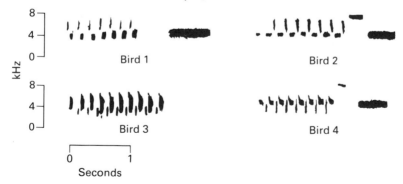

Fig. 4–6   Individually distinct songs of four male yellowhammers (1–4) in adjacent territories.

easier. However, the basic principle remains the same in that the signal should be constant whether repeated as a call or within the more complex structure of a song. There have been several attempts to identify the features responsible for individual recognition in passerine songs, and the most thorough is the work of BROOKS and FALLS (1975) on the white-throated sparrow (*Zonotrichia albicollis*). The approach depends upon establishing that territorial males have learned to recognize the characteristic songs of neighbouring males in adjacent territories. When males first occupy territories there is considerable aggression, and males tend to proclaim ownership by singing within their proposed territory. If a rival male sings near the newly established territory boundary, the resident male will sing back as well as approach, display and even attack if necessary. After several days the males will have staked out quite precise territory boundaries, and rivals learn where not to encroach upon their neighbours' territories. Singing may continue as a regular advertisement of territorial ownership or to attract a female, but overt aggression gradually decreases. This behaviour is considered to be adaptive, in that males would waste considerable time and valuable energy constantly responding to the songs of neighbouring males who are now established for a whole breeding season. It is suggested that males must *learn* not to respond to the particular songs of their neighbours who they have gradually come to recognize. As long as the *status quo* is maintained, each individual is now secure in his territory and free to concentrate upon more important activities such as feeding and breeding.

The hypothesis sounds quite convincing, but there are certain difficulties in testing for and interpreting negative responses during playback experiments. This was largely overcome by WEEDON and FALLS (1959) who developed an ingenious modification of the playback experiment originally involving the ovenbird (*Seiurus aurocapillus*), which was later extended to the white-throated sparrow and many other species. The first step is to demonstrate that each male gives a fairly weak response to songs recorded and played back from neighbours in an adjacent territory. Then songs recorded from a strange male some distance away are presented in the same place, and a much stronger reaction is obtained. The *differential response* is taken as evidence that the resident male cannot only discriminate between the two but recognizes the stranger as a threat to his territory and responds accordingly. It follows that the neighbour must be *recognized* as an established individual who now poses no threat and the response remains minimal. The response is measured using the usual variety of criteria such as response latency, nearest distance to speaker, and so on. In the white-throated sparrow example shown here (Fig. 4–7a) FALLS and BROOKS (1975) used the rate of singing in reply, and the difference in response between neighbours' and strangers' songs can be clearly seen both during and after the experiment. Gradual learning not to respond to a regularly repeated and constant stimulus is a well-known phenomenon in behaviour called *habituation*. If the properties of the stimulus vary in any way, the original response may return, and this is what happens when a new song suddenly appears. This general property may well have played an important role during the evolution of more complex song structures as we will see later.

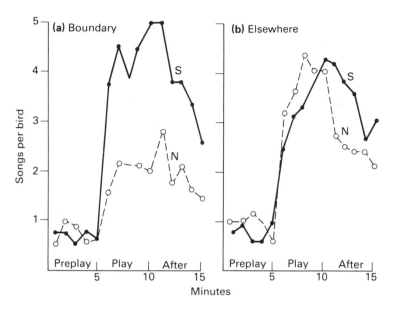

Fig. 4–7 Singing responses of male white-throated sparrows to playback of songs of neighbours (N) and strangers (S). (a) Speaker positioned on normal territory boundary with neighbour; (b) speaker positioned elsewhere on territory boundary (From FALLS and BROOKS, 1975.)

In this experiment, the playback speaker was placed on the territory boundary of the resident bird, in the position that the neighbouring bird might normally sing from. It could be argued that such recognition is not necessarily based upon the individual structure of the song, but merely upon recognizing neighbours' songs in general as opposed to strangers. If this is so, then by playing back a neighbour's song from a *different territory* elsewhere, on the opposite side of the resident male's territory from which it is normally heard, then we would expect the same weak response. But as Brooks and Falls showed (Fig. 4–7b) this is not the case and the new location produces a high response, the neighbour now being treated as a stranger. This suggests that males *learn* not only each neighbour's *individual song*, but also their normal *position*. A sudden change in position might mean that the neighbour is extending or changing his territory, the *status quo* is threatened as with a stranger, and the male reacts accordingly to defend his own boundaries with renewed vigour. By being able to identify neighbours, monitor their positions, and detect any new arrivals, the males are in a position to take quick, effective action only where and when it is really necessary. Valuable time is saved and energy conserved for other important tasks, and the risk of injury or even death in fighting unnecessarily is avoided. The *differential response* to neighbours' and strangers' songs was also utilized by BROOKS and FALLS (1975) in an experimental attempt to elucidate the features important for individual recognition in the white-throated sparrow. The songs are relatively simple in structure, consisting of a short series of fairly constant frequency whistles (Fig. 4–8). These constant pure tones within a certain

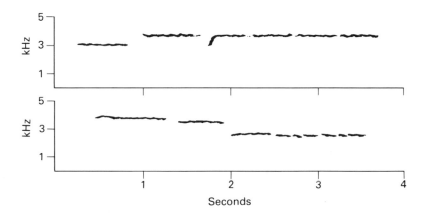

Fig. 4–8   Individually distinct songs of two white-throated sparrows. (From BROOKS and FALLS, 1975.)

frequency range and their temporal patterning appear to be important for species recognition. Each individual has more subtle variations in frequency within these constraints and these may form the basis for individual recognition. Human observers can often identify individuals by their different whistle patterns which remain constant from year to year. In a series of playback experiments, neighbours' songs were subtly altered until males failed to recognize them and responded as if to a stranger. Altering the frequency slightly within 5 to 10% was enough to lose recognition, but altering temporal patterning by similar amounts had no effect. The *individual information* appears to be contained in the *frequency pattern* of the first few elements, as recognition still occurs even after the remainder have been removed.

  In summary, the parameters of song involved in individual recognition should *vary between* individuals but remain *constant within* each individual. This is clearly different from species recognition where the parameters should not vary but remain *constant between* individuals. MARLER (1960) has pointed out that there appear to be conflicting selection pressures acting upon song structure, constancy being favoured to promote efficient species recognition, and variation to enhance individual recognition. He has suggested that the conflict may be resolved by relegating specific and individual information to different parameters of the same song, for example specific information in timing and individual information in frequency changes. To some extent, this is just what appears to occur in the case of the white-throated sparrow, where timing is important for species recognition but not for individual recognition. However, frequency changes appear to be important for both, and yet in rather different ways. Although pure tone whistles within a general frequency range appear to be critical for species recognition, more subtle frequency variations within the first few elements also carry the individual identity of the singing bird.

4.3   The functions of song

It appears that song can carry at least two types of information concerning the specific and individual identity of the singing bird. Other types of information may also be contained within the signal, but to whom is this information directed and why is it transmitted, or put simply, what are the possible *functions* of song? With calls, this question was often much easier to answer, as many are only used in a particular context and can be seen to have some immediate effect upon the behaviour of other individuals. In his book, ARMSTRONG (1973) has used a similar contextual approach to classify them as territorial, courtship, incubation songs, and so on. Some species certainly do have special songs which they only use in certain situations. For example, many warblers have a short, quiet, nest-relief song which they use to call their mate off the nest during a change-over in incubation. But these special songs are relatively unusual, and we are really concerned with the normal, loud, persistent advertisement so characteristic of the typical song bird. This is what Armstrong and indeed many others call '*territorial song*', because it is normally only produced by males in territory. It may well be a misleading term, as it also implies that song has solely or predominantly a territorial function, which may not be the case. In the wild it may occur as an apparently spontaneous, diurnal rhythm, a regularly repeated signal which may be influenced by various environmental factors such as the presence of other individuals. Even under artificial conditions it persists and has made isolated, caged song birds popular household pets in many parts of the world. Its very persistence and occurrence in a wide variety of immediate contexts has made the task of accurate functional interpretation extremely difficult in most cases. One way round this has been to extend the contextual correlation technique and look for long-term relationships instead of immediate ones. In most species there is a correlation between the onset of singing activity and the breeding season. Two important events happen at this time, the male must establish a territory and also find a female for breeding. This had led to a generally accepted view that song is concerned with obtaining either a territory, a mate, or perhaps both. The latter possibility has led many workers to suggest that song may have a *dual function*, to attract *females* and also to repel rival *males*. In one or two cases it has been claimed that these separate functions have been delegated to two structurally distinct song types, but these cases are unusual, and in the majority of species we are left with the difficult task of attempting to tease apart the relative importance of mate attraction and territorial advertisement in their songs.

The attraction of a female by song seems such an obvious function of an almost exclusively male signal, and yet there is surprisingly little direct or experimental evidence for it. The difficulty is that most male song birds take up a territory and then commence singing, making it impossible to clearly separate territorial from sexual advertisement. There is, however, a considerable body of more indirect, contextual evidence which does support the view that in many species song is of prime importance for *sexual attraction*. Reed warblers (*Acrocephalus scirpaceus*) are fairly typical song birds which take up territory in the spring and advertise their presence by considerable singing activity (CATCHPOLE, 1973). In these, and many other species, the unpaired male shows a characteristic, spontaneous, diurnal rhythm which can be accurately measured by counting songs or timing singing activity (Fig. 4–9). When a female is

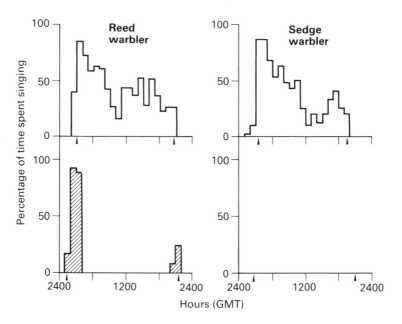

Fig. 4–9 Diurnal rhythm of song in a male reed and sedge warbler before (unshaded) and after (shaded) pairing. (Arrows indicate the approximate times of sunrise and sunset.) (From CATCHPOLE, 1973.)

attracted and pairing occurs, the amount of song decreases considerably, and is often restricted to the dawn and dusk chorus. There are two possible interpretations of this decrease in the normal diurnal rhythm. One is that if song is primarily a territorial advertisement, then the arrival of a female and pairing has merely interrupted the normal rhythm by placing new time or energy budget demands upon the singing male. He must now divide his time between singing and taking part in other activities such as courtship, nesting, incubation and feeding young. Another interpretation is that by this natural 'experiment' we have to some extent actually *separated* the territorial and sexual parts of the song display. The sexual attraction part has stopped because a female has been attracted, but the dawn and dusk territorial advertisement still continues. Further evidence of the direct inhibitory effect of the female is seen when she leaves the territory temporarily, in search of food or nesting material. The male invariably starts to sing, again, and if she deserts he will resume the normal diurnal rhythm until he attracts another female. This pattern is fairly typical of most song birds, but even stronger evidence for sexual attraction comes from species such as the closely related sedge warbler. Here the same natural experiment results in a dramatic and complete *cessation* of song after pairing (Fig. 4–9). It seems logical to suggest that in such cases song functions almost solely in sexual attraction.

Additional evidence that this is a real and functional interspecific difference comes from two sources. Observations show that if a rival male intrudes upon a reed warbler's territory, he will be repulsed by aggressive behaviour including song. The sedge warbler will also repulse rival males, but although the aggressive behaviour includes visual threat displays as well as actual fighting, *no singing* occurs. This has been further tested in playback experiments, when after pairing although both species respond aggressively by approaching the speaker, reed warblers invariably sing back whereas sedge warblers do not (see Fig. 2–3). The function of reed warbler song appears to be both territorial and sexual, whereas sedge warbler song appears to function almost solely for attraction of the female. The possible reasons for this difference between two such closely related species may be found in their rather different ecology. Reed warblers inhabit dense, impenetrable reed beds where vision is poor, and have small territories which need to be constantly defended by vocal means. In contrast, sedge warblers are more scattered throughout open, terrestrial habitats, where vision is good and less premium placed upon vocal defence. This may have led reed warblers to retain the territorial function of song, whereas sedge warblers were free to develop theirs for sexual attraction. There is additional evidence from the very structure of sedge warbler song that its elaboration is typical of the influence of sexual selection, but this will be discussed in detail later. The obvious playback experiment, to demonstrate male song attracts females, is more difficult than might be supposed. Female song birds are quiet, unobtrusive creatures difficult to observe at all, and the only result in most cases is to attract any males in the locality who are more than ready to defend their territorial boundaries. For the same reason, the standard playback experiment is of little value to the researcher who hopes to gain evidence that song is primarily important for territorial advertisement and actually repels other males.

Nevertheless, it is fair to say that considerable advances have been made recently by those seeking experimental evidence that song has a *territorial* function. It is common knowledge that territorial males sing against each other at the boundaries of their territories, and conventional playback experiments do show that song is used when invasion from a rival male is simulated. Whether or not the song itself actually repels a rival male is rather a different question which can only be answered by a more sophisticated experiment. One approach adopted by PEEK (1972) was to *stop normal song production* in territorial male red-winged blackbirds (*Agelaius phoeniceus*) and observe how this effected their territorial defence. He did this by trapping males and muting them by removing 2–3 cm of the hypoglossal nerves near the trachea. The operations were performed in the field, took one hour under anaesthetic, and the birds were left in their territories to recover. Control birds were operated on in identical fashion, but the nerves left intact. Although muted males had their territories invaded much more than normal singing controls, invaders were usually expelled by visual displays and actual attack. It seems that under normal conditions song acts as a *first line of defence* and does have a territorial function by initially discouraging potential invaders.

Much the same conclusion can be drawn from the very different experiments of KREBS (1976b) with the great tit (*Parus major*). Males tend to pair before taking up territory and singing, suggesting that in this species, song is more important in territorial advertisement than sexual attraction. Instead of using real birds and removing their song, Krebs removed territorial males and *replaced their songs* with a sophisticated system of loud speakers. The beauty of this experimental design is that it *isolates* the effects of song itself. Peek had the added complications of real birds, any abnormal noises they made, their colours, visual displays and attack to deal with, but here if any aversive effects are detected they can only be due to the *songs* played through the speakers. The experiments took place in a small six-hectare copse, normally occupied by eight territorial males. Early one morning, the males were all captured, removed, and three of the territories were each 'occupied' by four speakers and a tape recorder. Each recorder had a continuous tape loop containing eight minutes of normal great tit song, linked by a multiway switch to the four speakers placed in different parts of the territory. This pattern was designed to mimic the *normal singing behaviour* of a resident male each speaker being active in turn for two minutes, followed by a pause before the sequence starts again. This is just as though a resident male is regularly patrolling his territory, singing from several positions and pausing occasionally to feed. In the experimental design the wood also had two control areas, one of these being left completely silent as though empty. It could of course be that any experimental effect is merely due to the very presence of speakers in the wood or any unusual noises they may make. To control for this possibility, another area was also occupied by speakers playing a recording of a repetitive, two-note song from a tin whistle. The wood now contained three areas, the *experimental*, *control silent*, and *control sound* (Fig. 4–10). The whole system was switched on at dawn, the wood was visited every hour throughout the day and the positions of any new males seen and heard were plotted onto a scale map. Experiment 1 took place in February, and it can be seen quite clearly that after a few hours, only the control areas were occupied and the *experimental area avoided*. It could of course be that this is just the normal pattern of occupation in this wood, or that the control end is in some way much more attractive. To allow for this possibility the experiment was repeated in March, only this time the position of the experimental area was completely changed. Experiment 2 showed much the same result, it

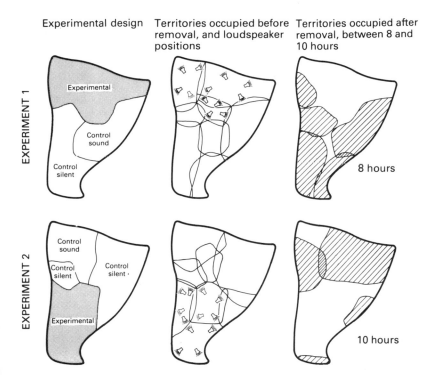

Fig. 4–10 Defending territories in a wood by recorded great tit songs. The resident males are removed, some territories 'occupied' by speakers, and the resulting pattern of invasion studied. (From KREBS, 1976b.)

was the experimental area the invading males avoided, no matter which end of the wood it was located in. In both experiments all the wood was completely occupied in about two days, but this experiment is certainly direct evidence that *song itself actually repels rival males* for some time. Under normal conditions, this first line of defence would be backed up by the appearance of the resident bird, visual threat displays, and if necessary overt aggression to defend the territory. Observations have long suggested such a sequence of events, but direct experimental evidence of the aversive effects of song itself has been lacking until now.

Attracting females and repelling rival males may well be the most important functions of song, but there is also evidence that superimposed on these are other more subtle effects upon the listening bird. We have already seen that male white-throated sparrows may learn the identities and positions of territorial neighbours by their songs and may habituate to them. In those species which attract a female by song most continue to sing to some extent after pairing, and far from being a territorial advertisement it may well be necessary to retain the female, particularly when neighbouring males are still in song. The seasonal production of male song is known to be under endocrine control largely by androgens secreted by the testes. Castration usually abolishes singing which returns upon injection of testosterone. Less well-established are the affects of male song itself upon the reproductive physiology of females, but there is now experimental evidence from several species. It appears that playback of male song may accelerate various aspects of *reproductive development*, both physiological, such as ovarian and egg development, as well as behavioural aspects, such as courtship or nest building. HINDE and STEEL (1976) used ovariectomized female canaries (*Serinus canarius*) previously injected with oestrogen so that the endocrine state was known. The birds

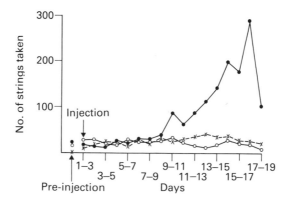

Fig. 4–11 Nesting activity in female canaries exposed to canary song (●———●), control budgerigar song (x – – – x), and no song (o———o). (From HINDE and STEEL, 1976.)

were kept under constant conditions of 12 hours daylight, but one group was exposed to playback of canary song, one to playback of budgerigar song as a control, and another to no song at all. One of the first signs of female breeding activity is nest building, and this was measured by providing each female with a hopper full of 10 cm lengths of white string. At the end of the day the strings taken were counted to give an accurate measurement of nest-building activity. After nine days the females in the canary song group showed a steadily increasing score compared to the control-song or no-song groups (Fig. 4–11). Their reproductive behaviour has clearly been stimulated and accelerated by playback of male canary song. It may well be that the sexual function of song is not only female attraction, but also synchronizing the reproductive behaviour of the mated pair and perhaps maintaining the strength of the pair-bond itself.

5 Song and Development

In many ways the study of song development in the individual bird has tended to parallel and reflect changing attitudes during the development of ethology itself. It has proved to be a fruitful area for experimental attempts to clarify the 'nature/nurture' or 'instinct/learning' debate which often dominated earlier writings of ethologists and their opponents. Initially, song was considered to be either wholly or predominantly innate, and there were claims that nestlings hand-reared in acoustic isolation produced quite normal songs when adult. Although many species do develop normal calls under such circumstances, passerines have complex songs and are extremely difficult to raise successfully in the laboratory from an early stage. To raise a bird in complete *acoustic isolation* the ideal method would be to incubate the eggs soon after laying, and thus remove any possibility of the embryo or newly hatched bird hearing and possibly learning adult song. In practice, most passerines are taken from the nest a few days after hatching and then raised by hand under various experimental conditions. Claims that 'isolated' young produce 'normal' song should be treated with caution, until we know exactly how isolated they were and at what stage they were taken, and until we can study recordings and sonagrams. A more direct way of removing any auditory feedback is to deafen young birds by *cochlea removal*, but this operation has to be done much later than the nestling stage. Yet another method is to *mask normal feedback* by rearing young with continuous 'white' noise, which contains sounds of every frequency.

In spite of these obvious difficulties, auditory isolation experiments soon suggested that learning and experience were extremely important in the development of normal song. The sterile nature of the 'instinct/learning' debate became obvious. Instead of taking up extreme positions about whether a behaviour pattern is innate *or* learned, the real question should be how does the behaviour *develop* in the individual? Whilst any behaviour must have a genetic basis it must also inevitably interact with the environment during development. The first step should be to study how the behaviour develops normally, and then to design isolation experiments which tease apart the relative importance of genetic and environmental components. The careful techniques and experiments which are needed still present certain problems, but at the same time continue to make important contributions to mainstream ethology. It now appears that whilst some species inherit an ability to learn a variety of possible vocal patterns, others are much more constrained and selective in what they are able to learn during development.

5.1   The development of song in the chaffinch

It was THORPE(1958a, 1958b, 1961) who pioneered the scientific study of song development in his classic work on the chaffinch. With the arrival of the sonagraph the fine details of song structure could be studied in an objective, qualitative way as never before under both natural and experimental conditions. Although the experiments are of great importance, we must first consider the pattern of normal song development in wild and captive birds. Soon after hatching in May young chaffinches give begging calls which stimulate the parents to feed them. Even at this early stage it is quite probable that the young nestlings may hear adults singing nearby. After fledging these calls develop into a crude, rambling kind of song called *subsong*, which differs from full song in a

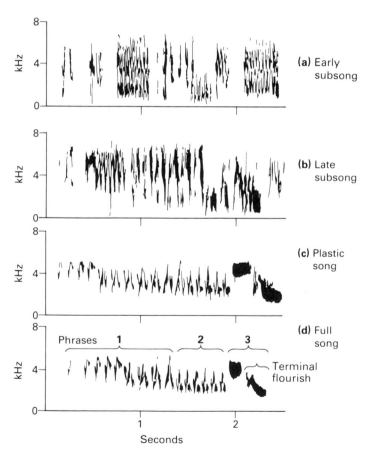

Fig. 5–1   Normal development of song in the chaffinch. (From THORPE, 1958b.)

number of ways. It is very quiet, with a wide frequency range and extremely variable in structure. Full chaffinch song has a stereotyped structure and lasts for only two or three seconds, whereas subsong can be much longer and consists of erratic bursts of chirps and harsh rattles (Fig. 5–1a). It appears to have no particular communicatory function and is probably best regarded as a practising stage, similar to the way in which young birds flap their wings before attempting real flight. Early subsong ceases in winter but reappears next spring when the young bird takes up territory for the first time (Fig. 5–1b). At this stage he is exposed to both the subsongs of other juveniles and also the full songs of adult males.

Later subsong becomes louder and more frequent, and every so often a quite passable version of a full song appears (Fig. 5–1c). These songs, sometimes called *plastic song*, are rather long, not clearly divided into phrases, and often contain the odd extra rattle or chirp. When a further process of 'tightening up' has occurred, and the *full song* is regularly repeated in exactly the same way, then the process is complete. Full song is characterized by being clearly divided into three parts or phrases (Fig. 5–1d). Phrase 1 consists of elements which gradually decrease in frequency, and can sometimes be further sub-divided into two parts. Phrase 2 is shorter and has a smaller number of elements of lower and quite constant frequency. Phrase 3 consists of a still smaller number of rather different and quite complicated elements, and the one which ends the song is called the terminal flourish. The situation is further complicated in that most birds will develop several different songs during this period, each with its own stereotyped structure. After about ten months each bird has a final repertoire of several different song types which it will use for its first breeding season. In future years a male may quickly pass through these stages each spring, but the final song types developed during the first year will remain the same for the rest of his life.

Thorpe took young chaffinches from the nest at about five days after hatching and reared them alone in acoustic isolation in special sound-proof cages. The song they eventually developed next spring was clearly abnormal (Fig. 5–2a). Although the length was about right there was little differentiation into different elements or phrases. This *isolate song* is probably quite close to the innate component of chaffinch song, although the bird in this experiment does obtain some *auditory feedback* from its own rudimentary song. How more auditory feedback can effect the final song structure was shown by rearing *groups* of nestlings in soundproof cages. Each bird now obtains auditory feedback from the others as well, and the resulting song, although still highly abnormal, is more differentiated and complex in structure with some suggestion of phrasing (Fig. 5–2b). Each member of the group develops this song structure and so each group develops its own particular version of chaffinch song which is quite unique. This suggests that in the wild young chaffinches have the ability to *learn* from other individuals that they hear. That part of this process starts well before spring was shown by catching wild juvenile birds in

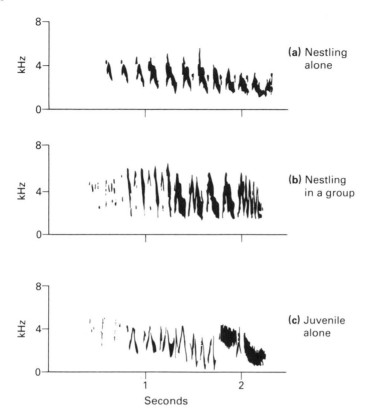

Fig. 5–2 Songs of chaffinches reared in auditory isolation from different stages. (From THORPE, 1958b.)

September, well before they are capable of producing plastic or full song, and subjecting them to the same type of experiment. In the spring, these birds developed songs which were almost normal (Fig. 5–2c) and have clearly learned from somewhere that songs should have three phrases and a terminal flourish. The implications of this experiment are that the juveniles have almost certainly heard and even learned some characteristics of adult song, some considerable time before they develop and sing their own songs. In the intervening months they have somehow stored or memorized a model of real chaffinch song, against which basis they will match and rapidly improve their first efforts in the spring. If any feedback from other birds is available at this stage it will also have an effect, and this was shown by juveniles raised in pairs. The first one to start singing is really an auditory isolate, but the second one hears this song and invariably copies that particular structure quite closely. In his final experiments Thorpe attempted to artificially control what songs the young birds heard in the first year. Hand-reared nestlings in auditory isolation were exposed to a few days of tape-recorded adult song in autumn, and in the following spring produced almost normal versions of it.

NOTTEBOHM (1968, 1970) extended Thorpe's early work by *deafening* chaffinches at various stages of song development by cochlea removal. This technique has the effect of *completely* removing auditory feedback whereas the intact bird reared in a sound-proof cage still obtains auditory feedback from its *own* vocalizations, however inadequate they may be. As might be expected the resulting songs were even more abnormal, and as a general rule the earlier the young birds were deafened, the more abnormal their adult songs. Nestlings taken at about five days after hatching, kept in sound-proof cages and then deafened after three months, produced songs almost totally lacking in pattern and described as a continuous screech (Fig. 5–3a). The considerable difference between this and the songs produced by more conventional auditory isolation must presumably be due to the absence of auditory feedback from the birds own song. Chaffinches deafened at the plastic song stage showed a gradual deterioration in song structure (Fig. 5–3b), but those deafened after full song had crystallized showed no appreciable effects (Fig. 5–3c) and indeed maintained their adult song structure for several years afterwards.

The first few months of life are clearly the *critical period* for song learning in the chaffinch, and after the permanent laying down of song types no more will be added in the future. The end of the song-learning period may not be just age-dependent as it is also correlated with the first high levels of testosterone in the blood. If a juvenile male is castrated before coming into song, then the end of the critical period can be delayed for another year. When implanted with testosterone the yong male will now learn a song type a year later than normal. NOTTEBOHM (1971) has also found that plasticity during the critical period also extends to neural and motor control of song in the chaffinch. As mentioned previously (§ 1.1), the left hypoglossus appears to be dominant in normal adults and when sectioned most of the song elements are lost. If this operation is performed before song development the normally under-utilized right hypoglossus takes over and normal song is developed on that side instead.

5.2   Selective learning and neural templates

From work on the chaffinch, and later on other species too, it became clear that learning during an early critical period played an important role in the development of normal song. Under natural conditions the young bird would obviously be exposed to the song of its own species, but might also hear the songs of other species too. If the song-learning mechanism is completely flexible and not subject to any constraints, then

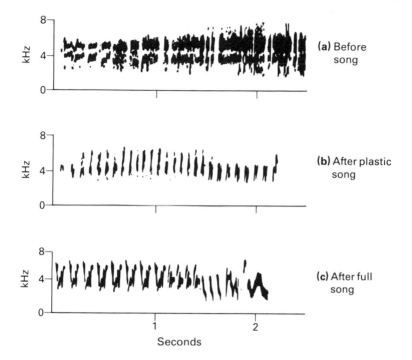

Fig. 5-3 Songs of chaffinches deafened at different stages in song development. (From NOTTEBOHM, 1968.)

the young bird might learn the song of another species or contaminate its own species song with alien elements. As we have seen in the previous chapter, most birds rely upon certain fixed parameters for species recognition and so such an individual would be at a serious disadvantage in intraspecific communication. Most species have therefore evolved song-learning mechanisms which have built-in constraints imposing some control upon what can and cannot be learned. This *selective learning* was also revealed by Thorpe during his chaffinch experiments. Having used recordings to tutor young birds during the critical period with normal chaffinch song, he also tried using a number of artificial and alien songs as well. However, these were only successful if their characteristics were similar to those in chaffinch song. For example, the tree pipit (*Anthus trivialis*) has a song which sometimes resembles that of the chaffinch and young birds tutored on this eventually produced quite a reasonable imitation. Real chaffinch songs re-articulated so that the terminal flourish appeared in the middle instead of the end were also used, and the young birds were able to learn these extremely well (Fig. 5-4).

MARLER and PETERS (1977) have recently investigated in some detail the basis of selective learning in song and swamp sparrows of the genus

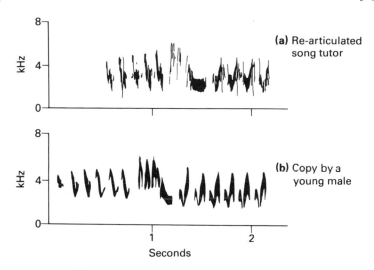

Fig. 5-4   Song tutoring with a re-articulated chaffinch song containing the terminal flourish in the centre. (From THORPE, 1958a and b.)

Melospiza. The songs of the two species differ particularly in temporal organization; swamp sparrows have a fairly regular, slow trill, whereas song sparrows have a more complex pattern of different fast and slow sections. Marler and Peters anticipated that these differences in temporal patterning might form the basis for any selective learning and to test their hypothesis constructed a series of artificial songs with which to tutor young swamp sparrows. These included swamp sparrow-like patterns, which were sequences of identical elements at a steady rate, and song sparrow-like patterns which had the more complicated structure of at least two different fast and slow parts. The young males were tutored with the various songs twice a day between the twentieth and fiftieth day after hatching, within the critical period for this species. When they eventually came into song several months later, only swamp sparrow songs had been learned. The young swamp sparrows had rejected song sparrow elements even when presented in swamp sparrow-like patterns, and the selective learning was clearly based upon the *specific structure of the elements*, not their temporal patterning as first thought. By fostering swamp sparrow eggs into canary nests, Marler and Peters also demonstrated that this early disposition for selective learning occurred without the possibility of earlier auditory experience. The experiments were repeated with these more thorough isolates who had no opportunity to hear their species song even as embryos. A similar pattern of results confirmed what appears to be an inherited basis for selective learning in this species.

However, not all species are subject to the same type of constraints, as shown by IMMELMANN (1969) in his work on tropical grass finches such as the zebra finch (*Taeniopygia guttata*). The advantage of working with zebra finches is that in captivity they can be readily fostered upon other closely related species such as the Bengalese finch (*Lonchura striata*). Single eggs of one species were added to the clutch of another species and the brood reared in a sound-proof cage. At various stages the fostered young were then isolated in other sound-proof cages until their song developed. Young males separated after 80 days invariably developed the song of their *foster father* even though he was a quite *different species*. Just how complete and accurate the copying is, can be seen from the song of a young zebra finch raised with a Bengalese finch foster father (Fig. 5–5).

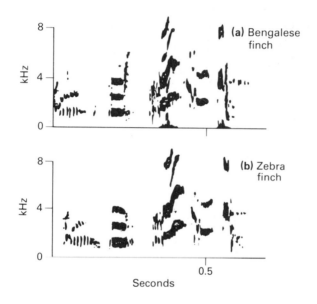

Fig. 5–5   Song of a Bengalese finch foster father and the young zebra finch it raised. (From IMMELMANN, 1969.)

Such individuals can then be housed with fellow zebra finches singing normal songs, but they still persist in singing Bengalese finch songs. Even though the critical period is shorter and the song of another species learned, once the process is complete it appears to be irreversible, as with other species. Why zebra finches are not so selective in the types of songs they will learn may be explicable in terms of their ecology and breeding behaviour. Unlike passerines in temperate latitudes they sing and breed throughout the year, often in colonial conditions and frequently near other species of grass finch too. Under these conditions, the best strategy for song development might well be to learn the species song quickly from the father before going off to feed in mixed-species flocks where the risk of contamination would be high. The constraints here are applied through social bonding and a quick end to the critical period, rather than through an inherited preference for learning a specific song as in most other passerines.

As a final example and a summary, we will consider the case of the white-crowned sparrow (*Zonotrichia leucophrys*) whose song development has been studied in detail by Marler and others. The findings in many ways support those from the chaffinch studies, but one difference is that the critical period for song learning is considerably shorter and finishes after about 50 days. MARLER (1975) has reviewed the various studies and summarized and interpreted them in terms of a *neural template* hypothesis (Fig. 5–6). We know that the songs of birds reared in auditory isolation still retain some specific characteristics, but that these are normally learned during an early critical period and somehow remembered or stored until full song is produced months later. The hypothesis suggests that an inherited, but modifiable, template is located somewhere in the neural pathways to which the bird can eventually match its vocal output by auditory feedback. The template appears to be highly selective in such species as the white-crowned sparrow for whilst it accepts its own species song as a model, it rejects those of other species such as the song sparrow which have a different song structure (Fig. 5–6A). When exposed to the model adult song in the first few days this improves the template, which in the case of the white-crowned sparrow may even include the specifications of the local dialect. This is now stored for at least 100 days until subsong begins when vocal output is gradually improved to match the dialect specified by the improved template. Eventually this crystallizes into full song which is a close copy of the model learned during the critical period. In an isolation experiment (Fig. 5–6B), no model is provided and what we see in the eventual song is presumably a representation of the innate, unimproved template. Vocal output still attempts to match it during development and so a few species qualities may persist in the final abnormal song. The hypothesis also explains why deafening produces an even more abnormal song, as it renders the template inaccessible for matching vocal output against even its unimproved form. There is as yet no direct evidence that neural templates actually exist in one or several parts of the nervous system, but the hypothesis does fit the available experimental evidence and at this stage certainly provides a useful way of summarizing and unifying the many observations and experiments into a plausible model of song learning.

5.3   The development of dialects

Human beings are well aware that although the people of any one country may share the same basic language, there are local variations in speech from place to place called dialects. Much the same phenomenon occurs in bird songs, but it is usual to distinguish between local dialects

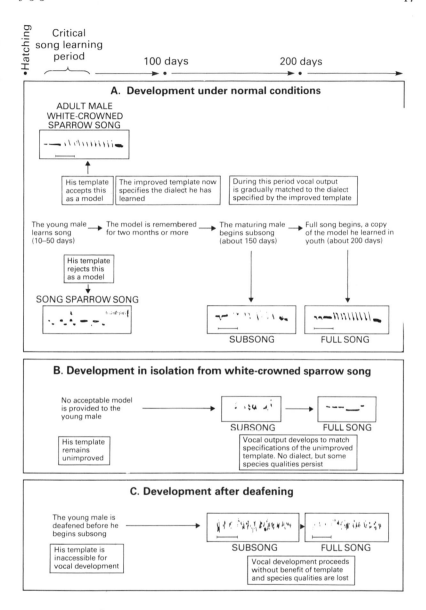

Fig. 5–6 Diagrammatic representation of the template hypothesis for song development in the white-crowned sparrow. (From MARLER, 1975.)

and *geographical variation* which occurs over long distances between populations which do not normally interbreed. Local *dialects* occur when the songs within one population are similar but differ from other populations nearby with whom interbreeding could easily occur. Geographical variation and dialects have been studied in many species and more examples can be found in the book by THIELCKE (1976). Perhaps the best known example of a dialect occurs in a bird we have just considered, the white-crowned sparrow. Just as linguists, like the famous Professor Higgins, can place a human being within a few kilometres of home by voice alone, so can ornithologists with the white-crowned sparrow around San Francisco Bay. The species is ideal for dialect studies as each individual has only one song type. The songs are also relatively short and simple, consisting of one or more introductory whistles, followed by a trill and sometimes a harsh buzzing element as well.

MARLER and TAMURA (1964) obtained sonagraphic evidence of clear dialects based upon variations in the pattern of introductory whistles, the fine structure of the trill, and the position of the buzz (Fig. 5–7). The population at Berkeley, for example, has three or more ascending introductory whistles, that at Marin has one or two with a terminal buzz, and that at Sunset Beach has two ascending or two followed by a buzz. There are other consistent differences in the fine structure of the trill which make this an excellent example of how individuals within each population conform to the dialect for their particular area. The question arises as to how this conformity comes about, and the answer lies in what is already known about the development of song in the white-crowned sparrow. Marler and Tamura took nestlings as well as young birds from the wild at up to 100 days old and raised both groups in acoustic isolation. The nestlings eventually produced abnormal songs which bore no relation to their home dialect, whereas the older wild trapped birds produced good copies of their dialect. This suggests that the special features of dialects are not inherited but *learned* with the general features of the species song. Marler and Tamura confirmed this by tutoring young birds during the critical period and showed that they could learn their own or even a 'foreign' dialect at this time. Whilst the neural template rejects the songs of closely related species as a model, it is clearly flexible enough to accept different varieties of the species song. With the critical period in the white-crowned sparrow ending as soon as 50 days, it seems highly likely that the model will be either the song of the father, or a neighbouring male, and thus the local dialect is preserved and passed on by a form of *cultural transmission*.

We can explain how dialects are self-perpetuating as a result of song learning, and how they may arise during the colonization of new areas will be discussed in the final chapter. Song learning itself may have evolved in birds such as passerines which have complicated song structures, and cultural transmission is possibly the best way of passing these on to successive generations. However, the question that still

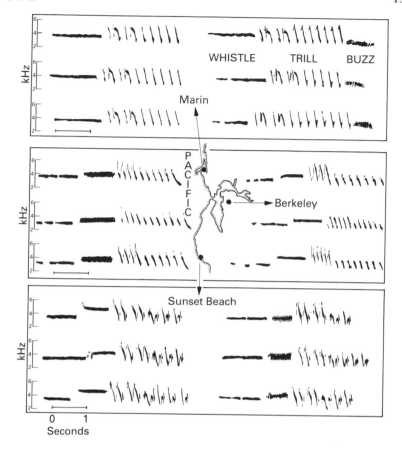

Fig. 5-7   Songs of 18 male white-crowned sparrows from three different dialect areas around San Francisco Bay. (From MARLER and TAMURA, 1964.)

remains is, are dialects merely a functionless by-product of song learning, or do they have some additional role to play in communication? There are many theories concerning the significance of dialects, but perhaps the most interesting to emerge is that they may be involved in reducing *gene flow* between populations. NOTTEBOHM (1970) has pointed out that dialects are sometimes associated with different habitats, as well as populations, and suggested that dialects might attract only those females which are best adapted to breed in local conditions, thus making adaptation to a particular habitat more efficient. Several predictions follow from such a theory: local populations are genetically different, these differences are adaptive, there is reduced gene flow between populations, and females select males which sing their own dialect. In the white-crowned sparrow there is some evidence from playback experiments that both males and females show a stronger response to their own dialect, but more information is needed about assortive mating under natural conditions. BAKER (1975) has used electrophoretic analysis of proteins from presumptive genetic loci to demonstrate that there are greater genetic differences between populations of white-crowned sparrows which also have dialects, and that gene flow appears to be reduced between them. This is an extremely interesting development, but clearly an area where more research is needed before the full significance of dialects is understood.

6 Song and Evolution

Ethologists believe that an animal's behaviour, like its structure, has been shaped by the forces of natural selection and so the vocalizations we hear now are the result of thousands of years of evolution. We have already seen how vocalizations have become adapted to communicate many different types of information, and in a sense this whole book has been concerned with the evolution of an efficient communication system. However, there are still many questions which remain and this final chapter will attempt to answer some of them, or at least outline a few of the unresolved problems. In particular, we will be concerned with the central problem of why songs have become so complex during evolution, as well as how they originate and are then passed on to successive generations.

6.1 Some evolutionary constraints

The design and evolution of any communication system is limited by certain constraints, and in birds their size and structure do impose restrictions upon the types of vocalization which can be produced. For example, it is physically impossible for many small birds to produce very deep, low-frequency sounds with such small equipment. As well as such rather obvious constraints, there are those imposed by the particular *habitat* each species occupies. The inverse-square law predicts that higher frequencies will attenuate more with increasing distance, but this is without the added complication of vegetation which tends to absorb frequencies differentially. What can be said is that all frequencies do not propagate equally well in any given habitat and therefore selection should favour the development of those which attenuate less and propagate furthest. MORTON (1975) carried out sound-propagation tests in different habitats and found that in forest a comparatively narrow frequency range of between 1.5 and 2.5 kHz showed less attenuation. He then examined the frequency ranges of forest birds and found that the average frequency used was within this narrow window at 2.2 kHz. The songs also contained more pure tones, so concentrating the sound energy within the narrow frequency range most suitable for effective propagation. At the edges of the forest a wide range of frequencies showed similar attenuation, and he found that the birds here used a much wider frequency range in their songs. In open grassland habitats there are the additional hazards of more variable atmospheric conditions, such as air turbulence which tends to distort frequencies. The birds here were found to avoid pure tones and instead rely more upon temporal coding of information in frequency modulations.

Songs must also evolve against a general acoustic background, including the songs produced by their own and other species. Having found the optimal frequency range to transmit there may well be *competition* for it. The most obvious source of direct competition is from other individuals of the same species. but this may be reduced to some extent by spacing out as in territorial behaviour. Individuals of some species have been found to wait until near neighbours stop singing before starting themselves, but most are just as likely to engage in counter-singing with a neighbour or even join in the general chorus. In some cases, species which share the same habitat may avoid the possibility of masking each other by having different diurnal patterns of singing activity. But serious interference seems most unlikely as in many cases direct competition is avoided by *evolutionary divergence* in song structure. MARLER (1960) in particular has pointed out that when sympatric species occur, selection will favour divergence to promote effective species recognition and maintain *reproductive isolation*. That songs are good indicators of species has long been known, and the early English naturalist Gilbert White of Selborne pointed out that with small warblers the distinct songs were usually more reliable than the similar plumage. Even in cases where the songs sound similar to human ears, the sonagraph reveals significant differences which would be detected by the superior resolving powers of the avian ear. For example, the grasshopper warbler (*Locustella naevia*) and Savi's warbler (*L. luscinoides*) produce a similar insect-like buzzing noise, but THORPE (1961) showed by sonagraphic analysis that the former consisted of about 30 triple pulses and the latter about 50 double pulses a second. Another example are the *Acrocephalus* warblers which also produce continuous, similar-sounding songs, but this time much more complicated in structure. Nevertheless, sonagraphic analysis (CATCHPOLE, 1978) reveals that each species has its own characteristic elements (Fig. 6–1) and there are also important differences in temporal and sequential organization. Playback experiments can be used to confirm that territorial males are not confused and do not respond to the songs of closely related species. In some cases, such as the *Acrocephalus* warblers, instances of one species also responding to the song of another are obtained, but there is an explanation which involves sympatry and interspecific competition.

Sedge warblers arrive first in the breeding areas and occupy territories. Reed warblers arrive later, but as there is a degree of overlap in ecological requirements, some try and oust the resident sedge warblers. The sedge warblers resist and there are instances of interspecific aggression where territories are defended against both species. Observation of what has become known as *interspecific territorialism*, coupled with a knowledge of the extent of ecological overlap, makes possible an interpretation of interspecific responses to playback in terms of evolutionary ecology. The sedge warbler is responding to both species because they are both ecological competitors to some extent. Whatever survival value accrues

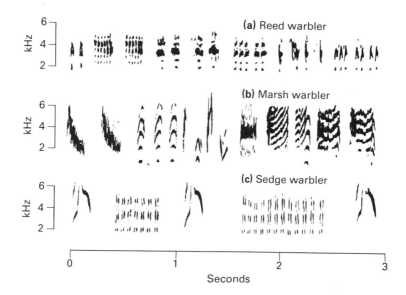

Fig. 6–1 Different song structures in three *Acrocephalus* warblers. (From
CATCHPOLE, 1978.)

from excluding males of the same species is similar in ecological terms to
that obtained from excluding a competitor of another species and will be
selected for during evolution. The fact that interspecific responses in
Acrocephalus warblers only occur in conditions of sympatry, and not in
allopatry, further supports the view that they are related to conditions of
competition and not confusion. Interspecific responses also tend to be
more variable and less predictable, and it may be that they are the result of
an individual's past experiences with the competing species. Bearing in
mind that some species can learn the songs of neighbouring territorial
males, it seems quite likely that they could also learn to recognize and
react to the songs of another species which is regularly encountered in
competitive situations.

MARLER (1960) also suggested that the selection pressures which
maintain divergence among sympatric species might be relaxed in conditions of allopatry. He used the idea of *competitive release* to explain why
isolated species on islands sometimes have more variable and potentially
confusing songs. A logical development of this is that any differences in
song structure between two species should be smaller in conditions of
allopatry than in sympatry. However, so far this theory of *contrast
reinforcement* has received little support from really analytical studies, as
pointed out by THIELCKE (1969). Just how important the constraints
applied by other species are during the evolution of song still remains a
highly speculative but fascinating area for future study.

6.2   Elaboration, redundancy and repertoires

One of the features which distinguish songs from calls is that songs are more elaborate in structure, and yet why such complexity has been selected for in evolution is still far from clear. In Chapter 3 we have seen how one relatively simple call is quite capable of carrying the various items of information (species, identity, location, etc.) that birds normally transmit during vocal communication. Indeed, it is only the oscine songbirds which have evolved such complicated signals, and most other birds manage to occupy territory, attract a mate and breed successfully without using a complicated song at all. Furthermore, songbirds do not appear to indulge in more sophisticated behaviours which might require the parallel development of more elaborate signals. There are two main possibilities which might explain the evolution of more complex songs. Either they transmit the *same* types of information *more effectively*, or they really do contain *additional information* which is advantageous and which we have so far been unable to detect.

In the former case, there is a certain amount of evidence from communication theory that the great redundancy in bird songs leads to more efficient information transfer. By *redundancy* a communications engineer means that some of the signal can be removed without reducing the information content, so that in spite of considerable interference or distortion the message still gets through. One way of achieving this is repetition which is a common feature of many bird songs. Indeed, it is possible to construct a plausible hypothesis concerning the evolution of songs from simply repeating single calls or elements. Some species may well have done this, for example the *Locustella* warblers just mentioned, and the Bonelli's warbler (see Fig. 4–3). A certain amount of repetition may well be advantageous within a song, although of course much the same could be achieved by merely repeating a call. But repetition is not the only form of redundancy, there is also the apparently functionless proliferation of different elements, sometimes to an enormous extent. They appear redundant because many species do not have such variety, and those that do, do not appear to use them in any additional way. BREMOND (1968) was able to remove and substitute many whole phrases from the robin's song without decreasing its effect in playback experiments and commented upon the apparent high redundancy of the elaborate song. Clearly redundancy, and any increased efficiency it may confer, is in itself unlikely to account for the extraordinary complexity of many songs. Indeed, far from promoting efficiency, such enormous elaboration seems more likely to confuse species or individual recognition, which makes its selective advantage even more puzzling. Celebrated elaborate songsters, sometimes called continuous singers, are far from unusual and can be found among such groups as thrushes, wrens, mockingbirds and warblers, and as an example of extreme elaboration we will consider the song of the sedge warbler (CATCHPOLE, 1976).

A sample song from a male sedge warbler is illustrated in Fig. 6–2, where various rules for song composition can be observed. A song always begins with the same combination of elements which ended the preceding song. Sedge warblers have about 50 different types of elements in their songs, and only a few of these are shown (numbered as they first occur) in the songs illustrated in Fig. 6–2. It can be seen that type 23 and 7 are the two elements which are alternated at the end of song 5 and the start of song 6. However, these two elements are not presented in a stereotyped way as in the songs of most passerines but instead appear in a variety of patterns, or *variations* on the main theme which never repeats itself in quite the same way. After this introduction, five new elements (27, 16, 40, 34 and 20) are suddenly injected in rapid succession to form the middle of the song. The end section is composed of two of these, 40 and 20, which are selected out from the middle section. These go on to alternate in a similar variable way to the start section, and indeed form the start section to the next song. In the middle of the next song several more new elements will suddenly appear, and so on. These are the basic rules of composition, but given that this individual had nearly 50 different types of element to select from, the possible combinations and permutations become astronomical. Detailed analysis revealed that sequence relationships between the different elements were highly indeterminate, and it was impossible to predict which elements would be selected next. In spite of considerable searching of tapes, no two songs were ever found which contained even the same permutations of elements, and when just two were found together again as a theme, their variations were different. In other words, the sedge warbler has *no stereotyped song types* as in a chaffinch or yellowhammer, but instead composes a seemingly endless stream of constantly varying, unique song types. On top of this the songs are extremely long, they can last over a minute and contain several hundred elements. Even the spacing between two alternating elements is remarkably variable, and the probability of a song type ever being exactly repeated seems extremely remote. In searching for any possible advantages of possessing such an elaborate song, there is a significant clue in the way the sedge warbler uses his song (see § 4.3). In brief, there is considerable evidence he uses it almost exclusively for sexual attraction of the female and never sings again after pairing (CATCHPOLE, 1973). This suggests that *sexual selection* might well be the main evolutionary force responsible for this extraordinary elaboration. Darwin explained the elaborate plumages of peacocks in this way and we can think of sedge warbler song as a kind of acoustic peacock's tail. Modern evolutionary theory suggests that sexual selection operates best when there is intensive competition for mates or when males are polygynous.

KROODSMA (1977) has looked for correlations between mating systems of wrens and the complexity of their song structures. He found that, as a

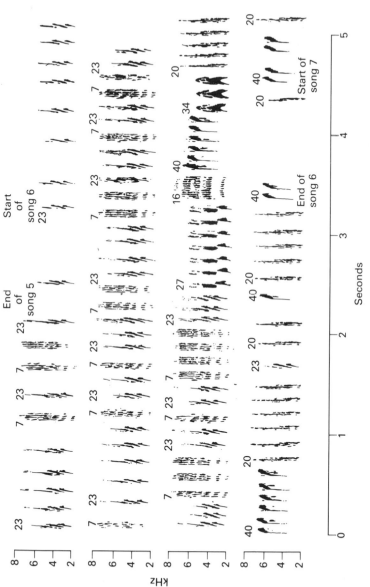

Fig. 6–2 Structure of a complex song (no. 6) in the sedge warbler. The end of the previous song (no. 5) and the start of the next song (no. 7) are also shown. (From CATCHPOLE, 1976.)

general rule, the more elaborate a species song the more likely the mating system was to be polygynous. But for sexual selection to work it must be demonstrated that females do *prefer* males with more elaborate songs which can therefore be said to be more attractive. HOWARD (1974) found that male mockingbirds (*Mimus polyglottos*) with more complicated songs obtained better territories and attracted females earlier. KROODSMA (1976) working on captive canaries, has obtained experimental evidence of a more direct effect of complex songs upon females. Females were exposed to experimental tapes of either simple songs containing only five element types, or complex songs containing as many as 35 element types. The females exposed to complex song came into breeding condition and laid eggs earlier than those exposed to simple songs. The sooner males can attract females and the earlier they can produce offspring may be a considerable *selective advantage*, and this experiment appears to demonstrate that females can be influenced by a more elaborate song. Again, it does not seem that the more elaborate songs are passing different information, but simply making the process more effective. DAWKINS and KREBS (1978) have taken this approach even further by speculating that increasingly elaborate songs with high redundancy are a form of persuasive advertising which might even have a hypnotic effect upon other individuals whose behaviour they are seeking to manipulate. Once a more elaborate song is selected by females which breed *more successfully*, their offspring will tend to produce and be attracted to more elaborate songs, and the characteristic runaway process of sexual selection will end up by producing the extraordinary complexities in song structures that we now find so difficult to understand in any other way.

The most elaborate songs have been considered first, in the hope that whatever factors are acting to promote elaboration might be more obvious in extreme forms. But even if sexual selection is primarily responsible for over-elaboration, there are still the majority of songs which in terms of complexity fall between the simple buzz of *Locustella* and the highly elaborate songs of *Acrocephalus* warblers. Most species, instead of having one or a nearly infinite number of different songs, have a relatively small number of highly stereotyped song types. The size of this *repertoire* varies from two to about twenty with repertoires under ten being more common. For example, each yellowhammer usually has two or three quite distinct song types (Fig. 6–3) and other well-known repertoire species mentioned earlier include the chaffinch and great tit. It might be thought that repertoires provide an ideal system for carrying different types of information, but efforts to establish that different song types are correlated with different functions have met with little success. In most cases the different song types appear to be used in the same context, and indeed one characteristic of classic repertoire species is rapid switching from one song type to another. During normal singing one song type is repeated a few times before switching to another, which is also repeated several times, and so on. Repertoires are certainly characterized by high

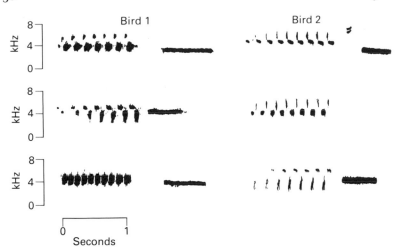

Fig. 6–3 The repertoires of two male yellowhammers each containing three different song types.

redundancy and there are many theories which attempt to explain their significance.

As before, sexual selection may be important, but there is little evidence for it, and instead rather more for the effects upon other males in territorial situations. For example, when rival males are engaged in territorial disputes they often sing vigorously against each other. During this the resident male will often attempt to match the song type produced by the intruder, if it is in his own repertoire. This *matched countersinging* in some species seems quite effective in driving off intruders, as if the resident male is conveying that he recognizes a particular challenge and is prepared to respond to it. But the system does depend upon sharing song types, and although this does occur to some extent, it is unlikely that any one male will have all the song types in his area, particularly in small repertoire species. Another way in which repertoires might be more effective in repelling rival males has been suggested by HARTSHORNE (1973) with his *monotony threshold* hypothesis. He points out that merely repeating a stereotyped signal is extremely monotonous and could be less effective due to habituation by the listener. KREBS (1976a) has indeed shown that male great tits do habituate more rapidly to playback of single song types than repertoires. In Chapter 4 we saw how he was able to demonstrate experimentally the aversive effect of song upon male great tits invading a wood. Now he has used a similar experimental design to show that repertoires are even *more effective* in this role than a single song type, (KREBS *et al.*, 1978). As before, the wood was 'occupied' by a system of loud-speakers and divided into three areas. The *control* area was left empty, another area was occupied by loudspeakers broadcasting a *single song type*,

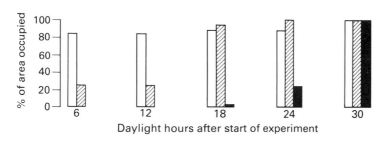

Fig. 6–4 Rates of occupation by male great tits of three areas defended by experimental songs. White = no songs (control); shaded = one song type; black = repertoire. (From KREBS *et al.*, 1978.)

and the final area by those broadcasting a *repertoire*. The results from one such experiment are shown in Fig. 6–4. It can be seen that whereas the control area was occupied almost immediately, and the single song area soon after, the repertoire area was occupied last of all. Krebs has suggested that prospecting males normally listen to the songs of residents and, by using habituation as a mechanism for density assessment, avoid crowded areas which would be unfavourable for breeding. He has also put forward the intriguing suggestion that resident males might *cheat* the system by producing several song types and thus create the impression that the area is more crowded than it really is. Rival males will be discouraged from settling, so leaving the area less crowded and more favourable for successful breeding by the residents. Thus, acquiring a repertoire appears to give male great tits a selective advantage in at least one respect, but whether they are additional advantages in this or other repertoire species still remains to be seen.

6.3 Duetting and mimicry

Duetting is another case where evolution has favoured the development of complexity in song structure. In a duet, instead of the male singing alone, the female also contributes and the result is a specific song which contains within its structure elements from *both* individuals. The songs produced are usually quite stereotyped and the contributions of the two individuals so well coordinated and integrated that to the listener it seems to be produced by only one bird. A duet may only be clearly revealed when standing between the two birds, or under captive conditions when separate microphones can be used to separate the pair on two tracks of a stereophonic tape recorder. Duetting has been found to occur in many different groups of tropical birds (reviewed by THORPE, 1972), and one which has been particularly well studied are the African shrikes of the genus *Laniarius*. In some species, such as *L. erythrogaster*, the male produces one element and the female another in a simple alternating system called *antiphonal singing.* In other cases, such as *L. funebris*, elements are combined in rather more complex sequences as shown in Fig. 6–5, Here, usually three different elements are used and some may be repeated. Each pair has a small repertoire of different elements and develop their own particular pattern of duets from them. Other pairs may share the elements, but the combinations selected by each pair for their duets are usually distinct. Other species have developed even more complicated duets involving long sequences of different elements. Some of the elements are produced consecutively as in antiphonal singing, but others are produced simultaneously by both birds as revealed by sonagraphic analysis of stereophonic recordings. What controls the selection and sequencing of elements by each bird during a complicated duet, and their very precise coordination to within thousandths of a second, is not fully understood. For example, we do not know how much each partner influences the other or how much of the patterning and timing has become stereotyped within each bird.

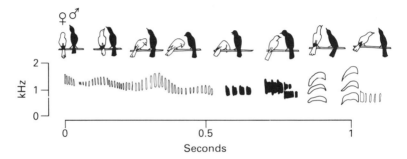

Fig. 6–5 Duet produced by a pair of African shrikes (*Lanarius funebris*). Black elements and birds are the male and white, female. (From SEIBT, WICKLER, 1977.)

Whilst the actual control and mechanics of duetting is certainly fascinating, so too are its possible functions. Once again we are faced with the problem of why such a complicated system should have evolved at all, but there may be clues to this in the distribution, ecology and behaviour of duetting birds. Although they are to be found in many different groups, they are almost exclusively tropical and often breed in fairly dense vegetation. They also tend to be resident rather than migratory, and so maintain a territory all the year round and for several years. They are usually monogamous and also maintain a pair-bond over several years and perhaps even for life. These correlations have led Thorpe and others to suggest that duetting may play an important role in maintaining the *pair-bond* over long periods of time in dense habitats where visibility is difficult. Certainly such conditions are conducive to the increased time, learning and familiarity which must be prerequisites to develop such a system. The birds must clearly learn their partner's elements and so be capable of individual recognition by voice when separated in a dense habitat. But if we look carefully at the context in which most duets are performed, it is in territorial encounters with rival pairs. Furthermore, as SEIBT and WICKLER (1977) have pointed out, duetting pairs invariably sit close together (Fig. 6–5) and yet the songs are extremely loud. Their measurements indicate that the songs are so loud that the conclusion appears inescapable that they are *territorial* proclamations directed at other pairs and not to each other. Evidence from playback experiments also supports this view. There are some quieter elements which do appear to be concerned primarily with communication between the mated pair, and just because the loud songs are used mainly for territorial defence does not mean that the pair are oblivious to them particularly when separated visually. We should be wary of making rash judgements concerning the ultimate factors involved in evolution based solely upon proximate evidence. It may well be that duetting evolved in rather special circumstances suggested by observed correlations, and for reasons not yet fully understood, under these conditions two now appear to be better than one, particularly in vocal defence of a territory.

An even more puzzling form of elaboration occurs in various forms of *vocal mimicry*. The Indian hill mynah (*Gracula religiosa*) is a well-known example which in captivity will learn to imitate the spoken words of its human captors, but in the wild it never mimics the sounds of other species (BERTRAM, 1970). Natural mimicry in the wild involves the regular or permanent incorporation of species-specific elements from the vocalization of *one* species into those of *another*. Why this has happened during evolution is difficult to explain, as in theory it would seem to promote confusion rather than efficiency in species recognition. However, in the case of brood parasites such as the viduine widow birds or whydahs of Africa, the advantages of mimicry seem more clear. All brood parasites lay their eggs in the nests of other species, which then hatch and feed the young as if they were their own. In cuckoos any visual mimicry only extends to the egg itself, and upon hatching earlier than the host eggs the young parasite ejects its rivals. The viduines have evolved a closer and much more subtle relationship with various species of estrildid grass finch whose nests they parasitize. Not only do they mimic the eggs, but also the young, which appear identical in terms of appearance and behaviour to the host young with whom they share the nest. Only after becoming independent, do the parasites moult into the true plumage of their own species. As described in the previous chapter, young estrildid finches, such as zebra finches, normally learn their adult songs from the parent while still in the nest. The young parasites also take advantage of this opportunity and they too learn the songs of the *host species*. The eventual *mimic* is an extremely good copy of the host *model*, as can be seen in Fig. 6–6. Young females also learn the host song and are attracted to it whether model or mimic. This is not so inefficient as it seems, as a viduine

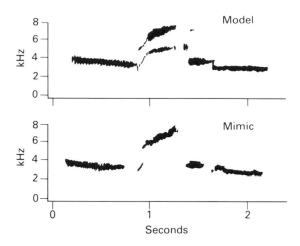

Fig. 6–6   Song mimicry of an estrildid finch (model) by a viduine paradise widow bird (mimic). (From NICOLAI, 1974.)

female must be able to find nests of the host species and synchronize her laying pattern with them so that the eggs hatch together. Reproductive isolation is maintained, for although females may be attracted by the same song, they will only mate with males who have their own species adult plumage. In this case, a flexible song-learning mechanism results in vocal mimicry which is used to cement even further the close association which has evolved between host and parasite.

However, most cases of mimicry involve species which mimic a bewildering *variety* of other species with which there is no apparent relationship at all. This category includes such celebrated mimics as starlings, lyrebirds and mockingbirds, but there are many less obvious mimics which are much harder to detect by ear. The *Acrocephalus* warblers, whose complex songs have been mentioned earlier, are also well-known mimics, but to varying degrees. The songs of reed and sedge warblers often contain elements which appear to be mimics of the calls of other passerine species. Sometimes these are obvious by ear alone, but suspected mimics should always be checked and matched by sonagraphic analysis. A good example is the loud and quite distinctive flight call of the yellow wagtail (*Motacilla flava*). Sonagraphic matching can never be perfect, but Fig. 6–7 shows how mimics by two *Acrocephalus* species closely conform to the distinctive triple structure of the model. (How this particular call is included as an element in sedge warbler song can also be seen in Fig.6–1.)

In reed and sedge warbler songs, such mimics are relatively scarce and account for only a small fraction of the total elements in the repertoire, while the song itself clearly maintains its specific distinctiveness. This is true for most *Acrocephalus* warblers, except for the highly mimetic and

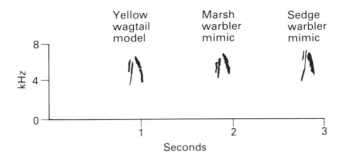

Fig. 6–7   Mimics of the yellow wagtail flight call by two *Acrocephalus* warblers.
(Model and marsh warbler mimic from LEMAIRE, 1975.)

quite extraordinary song of the marsh warbler (*Acrocephalus palustris*)
which has recently been painstakingly unravelled by LEMAIRE (e.g. 1975,
1979). The species had long been regarded as a celebrated mimic by
ornithologists but Lemaire, working in Belgium, went on to confirm by
sonagraphic analysis that about half of the repertoire consisted of
elements that were mimics of nearly 100 different *European* species. The
elements are copied extensively from the local bird community, for
example individuals from the coast have marine species in their
repertoires compared to those breeding inland. To have half a repertoire
'borrowed' from alien species is remarkable enough, so surely the
remaining half must consist of species-specific marsh warbler elements.
But marsh warblers breed in Europe then migrate to spend the winter in
central Africa, and Lemaire followed them to continue her studies there.
By the same careful detective work she has now established that most of
the unaccounted for elements are also 'borrowed' from over 100 different
species of the *African* avifauna. Because some of these are mimics of
species with an extremely local distribution, it may even be possible to
locate more accurately the autumn and winter quarters of the marsh
warbler. Only a small proportion of the total repertoire remains
unaccounted for, and as marsh warblers appear to copy indiscriminately
from local avifauna whenever they breed or travel it may be that we will
eventually learn the intricate details of their first migratory journey from
sonagraphic analysis of their repertoire. Lemaire believes that the
sensitive period for song learning ends quite soon in Africa, and as with
most other species no further elements are added after the first year. Each
individual mimics about 75 from over 200 species now identified as
models, and also prefers to use some more than others in songs. The
relative popularity of the twelve most common European and African
models in one individual's repertoire can be seen in Fig. 6–8. Because of
such variation Lemaire can identify certain individuals from their songs
alone.

How marsh warblers maintain *specific distinctiveness* with a song

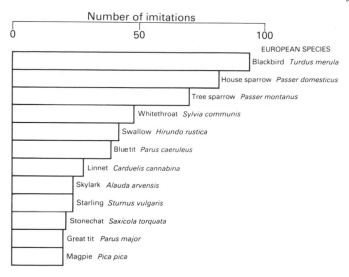

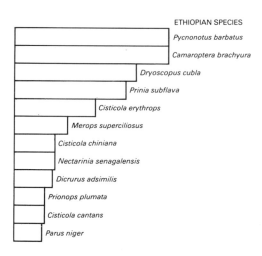

Fig. 6–8 Quantitative distribution of the 12 most commonly mimicked European and Ethiopian species recorded from one marsh warbler in 40 min of continuous song. (From LEMAIRE, 1979.)

composed almost totally of elements 'borrowed' from other species is less puzzling than might be supposed. In Chapter 4 we have seen that the 'rules' for species recognition vary tremendously from species to species. Although the marsh warbler appears to be totally unselective in what elements it will learn, Lemaire has shown that it uses them in a very characteristic pattern. No element is repeated for as long as in the model species, but instead different elements are mixed together and often alternated. The species-specific qualities of marsh warbler song are in the temporal and sequential *patterning* of the different alien elements, *not their individual structures*. The resulting song is a continuous stream of hundreds of constantly changing elements which is even more varied and complex than other *Acrocephalus* songs. We have already discussed the possible advantages of complexity in terms of reducing habituation by males or attracting females, and adding additional elements from other species is certainly one way in which a song may be made more elaborate. Evolving new elements may take time and perhaps one advantage of mimicry is the quick acquisition of elements which are ready-made. Why the marsh warbler has gone to such extremes is certainly intriguing, but by completely abandoning many of the normal constraints on learning this species has managed to find an efficient and rapid way of acquiring one of the most complicated and elaborate songs of all.

6.4   The origins of songs and cultural transmission

Even though many songs appear to be highly stereotyped and relatively unchanging in structure, they have presumably evolved from more simple ancestral forms. How this came about during evolution, perhaps by initially repeating simple calls, we can never be absolutely certain. There are, however, a number of ways in which new variations might arise, and some of these can be detected by analytical studies on living populations. We have already dealt with one method seen in the complex songs of *Acrocephalus* species such as the marsh warbler. Each male learns a selection of elements from other species, but combines them together in his own individual way. The sedge warbler uses mainly species-specific elements but again improvises with them to compose a host of new variations and combinations. Most species have more simple and stereotyped songs, but even here there is some scope for variation and the eventual development of a new song type. LEMON (1975) has suggested how this may occur through the re-arrangement of existing elements within a song, or even the development of completely new elements by a process called *drift*. Drift can be seen in the songs of many species such as the cardinal (*Cardinalis cardinalis*) (Fig. 6–9), where elements are often repeated. An element may show a gradual or more abrupt change in structure until a point is reached where quite a different element is eventually produced. Drift may involve changes in frequency or more extensive changes to the configuration of the original element. That such changes can be detected in the songs of living birds suggests that new varieties may be constantly appearing, but how do they become a more permanent part of a species repertoire or a dialect shared by the population?

The answer lies to a certain extent in what we already know about song

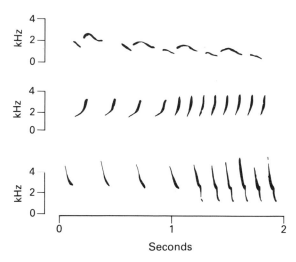

Fig. 6–9   Drift in the elements of songs from cardinals. (After LEMON, 1975.)

learning in the individual bird. As seen in Chapter 5, although subject to certain inherited constraints, most species learn their songs from other individuals and so songs are passed from generation to generation by a form of *cultural transmission*. What song types a young bird will learn depends upon several factors, such as the length of the sensitive period in relation to fledging and the first occupation of a breeding territory. There are two main sources of model songs, from the parents and neighbours round the nest, or from new neighbours surrounding the first breeding territory. Exactly how a young bird constructs his final repertoire from these sources is hard to say in many cases, but JENKINS (1978) has recently studied cultural transmission in an island population of saddlebacks (*Philesturnus carunculatus*). He found that there were relatively few song types on the island and these were usually shared by neighbouring males who could be grouped into dialect areas. When a young bird took up territory for the first time he learned his songs from neighbours, whether they were his parents or other individuals. During the study, Jenkins was privileged to actually witness the *origin* of completely new song types. These appeared to be the result of errors in the song-learning process, or *cultural mutations* as he calls them. They arose quite abruptly in an individual by changes in frequency, addition or deletion of an element, or a new combination of existing elements. For example, Fig. 6–10 shows the structure of one common 'ancestral' song type which has two low-frequency elements followed by one higher. One individual in the population suddenly produced a cultural mutation which added low-frequency components to the end element. This was then learned by other individuals and so started to spread through the population. The

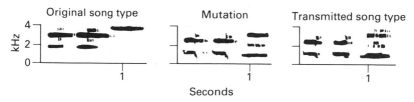

Fig. 6–10   Cultural mutation and transmission of song in the saddleback. (From
JENKINS, 1978.)

discovery of cultural transmission in a wild population of birds is
extremely interesting in its own right, but may also provide a clue to the
evolution of song learning itself. Cultural evolution is thought to proceed
at a much faster rate than genetic evolution, and the flexibility inherent in
song learning may well encourage the rapid spread of favourable vocal
adaptations in new or changing environments.

References and Further Reading

Books

ARMSTRONG, E. A. (1973). *A Study of Bird Song.* Dover Publications, New York.
HARTSHORNE, C. (1973). *Born to Sing.* Indiana University Press, Bloomington.
HINDE, R. A. (ed.) (1969). *Bird Vocalisations.* University Press, Cambridge.
JELLIS, R. (1977). *Bird Sounds and Their Meaning.* British Broadcasting Corporation,
London.
THIELCKE, G. (1976). *Bird Sounds.* University Press, Michigan.
THORPE, W. H. (1961). *Bird Song.* University Press, Cambridge.

Articles

BAKER, M. C. (1975). *Evolution,* 29, 226–41.
BERTRAM, B. (1970). *Anim. Behav. Monogr.,* 3, 81–192.
BREMOND, J. (1968). *La Terre et la Vie,* 2, 109–220.
BREMOND, J. (1976). *Behaviour,* 48, 99–116.
BROOKS, R. J. and FALLS, J. B. (1975). *Can. J. Zool.,* 53, 879–88, 1749–61.
CATCHPOLE, C. K. (1973). *Behaviour,* 46, 300–20.
CATCHPOLE, C. K. (1976). *Behaviour,* 59, 226–46.
CATCHPOLE, C. K. (1977). *Anim. Behav.,* 25, 489–96.
CATCHPOLE, C. K. (1978). *Anim. Behav.,* 26, 1072–80.
DAWKINS, R. and KREBS, J. (1978). In: KREBS, J. and DAVIES, N. (eds), *Behavioural Ecology.*
Blackwell, Oxford.
EMLEN, S. T. (1972). *Behaviour,* 41, 130–71.

FALLS, J. B. and BROOKS, R. J. (1975). *Can. J. Zool.*, **53**, 1412–20.

GRIFFIN, D. R. and SUTHERS, R. A. (1970). *Biol. Bull.*, **139**, 495–501.

GULLEDGE, J. L. (1977). *Living Bird*, **15**, 183–203.

HINDE, R. A. and STEEL, E. (1976). *Horm. Behav.*, **7**, 293–304.

HOWARD, R. D. (1974). *Evolution*, **28**, 428–38.

HUTCHINSON, R. E., STEVENSON, J. G. and THORPE, W. H. (1968). *Behaviour*, **32**, 150–7.

IMMELMANN, K. (1969). In: HINDE, R. A. (ed.), *Bird Vocalisations*.

JENKINS, P. (1978). *Anim. Behav.*, **26**, 50–78.

KONISHI, M. (1969). *Nature*, **222**, 566–7.

KONISHI, M. (1970). *Z. vergl. Physiologie*, **66**, 257–72.

KREBS, J. R. (1976a). *Behav. Ecol. Sociobiol.*, **1**, 215–27.

KREBS, J. R. (1976b). *New Scientist*, **70**, 534–6.

KREBS, J. R., ASHCROFT, R. and WEBBER, M. (1978). *Nature*, **271**, 539–42.

KROODSMA, D. (1976). *Science*, **192**, 574–5.

KROODSMA, D. (1977). *Amer. Nat.*, **111**, 995–1008.

LEMAIRE, F. (1975). *Le Gerfaut*, **65**, 3–28, 95–106.

LEMAIRE, F. (1979). *Ibis*, **121**, 453–68.

LEMON, R. E. (1975). *Condor*, **77**, 385–406.

MARLER, P. (1957). *Behaviour*, **11**, 13–39.

MARLER, P. (1960). In: LANYON, W. and TAVOLGA, W. (eds), *Animal Sounds and Communications*. American Institute of Biological Sciences, Washington.

MARLER, P. (1975). In: KAVANAGH, F. and CUTTINGS, J. (eds), *The Role of Speech in Language*. MIT Press, Cambridge, Massachusetts.

MARLER, P. and PETERS, S. (1977). *Science*, **198**, 519–21.

MARLER, P. and TAMURA, M. (1964). *Science*, **146**, 1483–6.

MORTON, E. S. (1975). *Amer. Nat.*, **109**, 17–34.

MOSS, R. and LOCKIE, I. (1979). *Ibis*, **121**, 95–7.

MUNDINGER, P. C. (1970). *Science*, **168**, 480–2.

NICOLAI, J. (1974). *Sci. Am.*, **231**, 93–8.

NOTTEBOHM, F. (1968). *Ibis*, **110**, 549–69.

NOTTEBOHM, F. (1970). *Science*, **167**, 950–6.

NOTTEBOHM, F. (1971), *J. Exp. Zool.*, **177**, 229–62.

PEEK, F. W. (1972). *Anim. Behav.*, **20**, 112–18.

SEIBT, V. and WICKLER, W. (1977). *Z. Tierpsychol.*, **43**, 180–7.

SHALTER, M. D. (1978). *Z. Tierpsychol.*, **46**, 260–7.

SHIOVITZ, K. A. (1975). *Behaviour*, **55**, 128–79.

SMITH, W. J. (1965). *Amer. Nat.*, **99**, 405–9.

THIELCKE, G. (1969). In: HINDE, R. A. (ed.), *Bird Vocalisations*.

THORPE, W. H. (1958a). *Nature*, **182**, 554–7.

THORPE, W. H. (1958b), *Ibis*, **100**, 535–70.

THORPE, W. H. (1972). *Behav. Suppl.*, **18**, 1–192.

THORPE, W. H. and GRIFFIN, D. R. (1962). *Ibis*, **104**, 220–7.

TSCHANZ, B. (1968). *Z. Tierpsychol.*, Beiheft 4.

VINCE, M. A. (1969). In: HINDE, R. A. (ed.), *Bird Vocalisations*.

WEEDON, J. S. and FALLS, J. B. (1959). *Auk*, **76**, 343–51.

WHITE, S. J. and WHITE, R. E. (1970). *Behaviour*, **37**, 40–54.

WILKINSON, R. and HOWSE, P. (1975). *Nature*, **258**, 320–1.